ANIMAL PLANET

Cats

KELLI A. WILKINS

Cats

Project Team
Editor: Mary E. Grangeia
Copy Editor: Stephanie Fornino
Interior Design: Leah Lococo Ltd. and Stephanie Krautheim
Design Layout: Angela Stanford

T.F.H. Publications
President/CEO: Glen S. Axelrod
Executive Vice President: Mark E. Johnson
Publisher: Christopher T. Reggio
Production Manager: Kathy Bontz

T.F.H. Publications, Inc.
One TFH Plaza
Third and Union Avenues
Neptune City, NJ 07753

Discovery Communications, Inc. Book Development Team
Maureen Smith, Executive Vice President & General Manager,
    Animal Planet
Carol LeBlanc, Vice President, Licensing
Elizabeth Bakacs, Vice President, Creative Services
Peggy Ang, Vice President, Animal Planet Marketing
Caitlin Erb, Licensing Specialist

Printed and bound in China.
09 10 11 12 13   3 5 7 9 8 6 4

Library of Congress Cataloging-in-Publication Data
Wilkins, Kelli A.
  Cats / Kelli A. Wilkins.
     p. cm. – (Animal planet pet care library)
  Includes index.
  ISBN 978-0-7938-3771-7 (alk. paper)
  1. Cats. I. Title.
SF447.W662 2007
636.8–dc22
   2006101386

This book has been published with the intent to provide accurate and authoritative information in regard to the subject matter within. While every reasonable precaution has been taken in preparation of this book, the author and publisher expressly disclaim responsibility for any errors, omissions, or adverse effects arising from the use or application of the information contained herein. The techniques and suggestions are used at the reader's discretion and are not to be considered a substitute for veterinary care. If you suspect a medical problem consult your veterinarian.

The Leader in Responsible Animal Care for Over 50 Years!®

www.tfh.com

Table of Contents

Chapter 1

Why I Adore My

Cat

Cats are found in all corners of the world and are cherished pets in homes everywhere. Domestic cats have been living with people for the last 6,000 years, and yet they've managed to retain their independence, natural instincts, and an aura of mystery. As any cat lover knows, they are unique individuals, with each one having distinct personality traits and behaviors.

Adaptable to almost any living condition, cats are easy to care for and make loving companions for people of all ages. With approximately 90 million cats living in American households today, the cat continues to be a popular pet. Most owners consider their cat to be a beloved member of the family.

The History of Cats

The domestic cats that we know today have a long history dating back millions of years. Paleontologists discovered evidence of a cat with retractable claws, *Miacis*, who lived about 50 million years ago. Most scientists believe that the descendants of *Miacis* and other prehistoric cats divided into three separate groups nearly a million years ago: the big cats (lions and tigers), the cheetahs, and the small cats (ocelots, bobcats, and lynxes).

Cats first started living with people approximately 6,000 years ago. Ancient Egyptian and Mesopotamian farmers domesticated the African wildcat, *Felis lybica*, a natural hunter, to keep grain storage areas rodent-free. Egyptians worshipped Bast, or Bastet—the cat goddess of fertility, happiness, and the moon. Impressed with the cat's natural beauty, Egyptian artists painted and sculpted them, making them cultural icons.

Although ancient Egyptians are known for their love of cats, they aren't the only people who worshipped them. In Thailand, Siamese cats were sacred temple cats, and in Japan, these animals kept Buddhist temples free of mice. In Norwegian mythology, Freya (the goddess of fertility) rode in a chariot pulled by two white cats. Cats made their way to China in 5,000 BCE and to India in 100 BCE.

Throughout history, sailors and other explorers helped spread cats across the world. They realized that keeping them aboard their ships was a good way to rid their living quarters of mice. In time, it was considered lucky to keep cats on board.

When cats came to Europe in 900 BCE, they crossbred with the

Breed Categories

Cats come in many shapes and sizes, but the fur coat found on each feline is a big part of how they are classified. They usually fall somewhere in the categories of long-haired, short-haired, or "hairless."
- Long-haired breeds include Persian, Himalayan, Maine Coon, Norwegian Forest Cat, and Ragdoll.
- Shorthaired breeds include American Shorthair, American Wirehair, Siamese, Burmese, Korat, and Singapura.
- "Hairless" cats, such as the Sphynx, merely appear to be hairless. The breed actually does have a thin layer of hair covering its body.

Found in all corners of the world, cats first started living with people approximately 6,000 years ago.

native cat found in the British Isles, *Felis silvestris*. By the Middle Ages, however, cats fell out of favor with most of Europe. The Catholic Church connected them and those who loved them with paganism, devil worship, and witchcraft. Superstitious people believed that cats (especially black cats) had diabolical powers. They were feared because of their nocturnal hunting habits, their ability to see in the dark, and their "glowing" eyes.

In 1484, Pope Innocent empowered the Inquisition to burn all cats and cat lovers. As a result of the drastic drop in the cat population, the number of rodents increased. Millions of rats carrying fleas infected with bubonic plague spread the Black Death across Europe. When the persecution of cats ended, they began hunting rats again,

and Europeans saw the advantage of having these natural hunters keep their towns rodent-free.

In Victorian times, they were once again warmly welcomed into the home and were seen as loving companion pets. Victorian cats impressed artists, writers, scientists, and philosophers of the day. Queen Victoria loved cats, and because of this, their good reputation was reaffirmed—where it remains to this day.

Physical Characteristics

Cats and kittens come in all shapes, colors, and sizes. Although approximately 100 different breeds exist, they all share the same basic body structure. Nature designed cats perfectly. Their bodies, sense organs, and natural instincts enable them to hunt and survive in the wild with

Why I Adore My Cat

no help from humans. Surprisingly, the domestic cat (*Felis domestica*) that we know and love today isn't much different from his wild "big cat" cousins—the lions and tigers. Although our house cats are much smaller in size (and cannot roar), they have retained many similar physical characteristics.

The Body

The average house cat measures roughly 30 inches (76.2 cm) from nose to tail and has approximately 244 bones. (The exact number of bones varies depending on the length of the tail.) Cats have 30 vertebrae in their spinal column, which make them incredibly agile and flexible. They can rotate half of their spine 180 degrees, seemingly bending themselves in half! These traits allow cats to leap great heights (they can jump five times their own height), sprint after prey, and climb trees easily. Felines have a great range of motion. They have no collarbone, and their shoulder blades are located close to their chest, which allows them to slip into narrow spaces. A cat's skin is loose on the body and functions as an anchor for the coat. It comprises millions of incredibly sensitive nerve endings, but it is not as sensitive to heat and cold as human skin is.

The Paws

Cats have five toes on their front feet (or forepaws) and four toes on their back feet. A kitten born with extra toes (anywhere from one to four extra toes per foot) has a condition called *polydactyly*. In most cases, the extra toes aren't a problem, but if they impede the ability to walk properly, the extra toes may need to be surgically removed.

The paws are very sensitive and are filled with nerves and touch receptors. Cats feel vibrations through the pads on their feet. These footpads are made up of thick, tough

Although approximately 100 different breeds of cat exist, they all share the same basic body structure.

Cat Myths

Because of their mysterious nature, many myths and old wives' tales circulate about cats. Here are a few of the more common ones—and the facts behind the fiction.

Myth 1: *A spayed or neutered cat will become fat and lazy.* Not true! A cat's weight gain is not related to his or her reproductive status. Any cat who does not get the proper amount of exercise or who is overfed will become overweight and sluggish. Spaying or neutering is beneficial to your pet. Cats and kittens who have been spayed or neutered live longer, don't stray from home, and become more affectionate.

Myth 2: *My female cat must have a litter of kittens before she's spayed; otherwise, she will become unfriendly.* False! Females who are spayed before they have kittens don't miss being mothers. In fact, some cats are not good mothers and may resent their kittens. One cat and her offspring can produce approximately 420,000 cats in seven years. With millions of unwanted kittens and cats euthanized in animal shelters each year, there is no reason to add to the pet overpopulation problem.

Myth 3: *Cats belong outside. Indoor cats suffer or become bored if they're never allowed to go outside to hunt and explore.* Not true! Indoor-only cats thrive in the home. Given the proper amount of attention and affection, your cat will not miss being outside. Cats and kittens can learn to walk on leashes to safely experience the outdoors, and most are content to observe nature from a window. Cats who are allowed to roam outside do not live as long as indoor cats because they are subject to many hazards, such as traffic, diseases, and toxic poisons.

Myth 4: *Cats always land on their feet when they fall.* This myth is partially true. Cats have excellent reflexes and can right themselves quickly. They have a flexible backbone, and as mentioned earlier, can rotate half of their spine 180 degrees. This trait, combined with a fluid-filled chamber in the ears, helps a cat to right himself if he falls. If a cat falls one or two stories, he usually will right himself and may only receive mild injuries. However, falling from three to six floors is usually fatal because the velocity from this distance is too great, although some cats have survived a seven- or eight-floor drop. In this circumstance, the extra time involved in the fall allows the cat to right himself, spread out his feet, and relax, thus creating drag resistance to slow him down.

skin that acts like a shock absorber and protects the feet while walking. The forepaws are made up of three sets of small bones that form a digit, much like the finger on a human hand. These specialized bones allow the cat to extend and retract his claws at will.

The Ears

Twelve different muscles control the pointed outer part of the ear (called the *pinna*). These muscles allow the cat to independently rotate the outer ears 180 degrees in any direction. The three canals located in the inner ear help to give the cat an excellent sense of balance. These chambers are arranged at right angles, allowing the brain to detect changes in direction or speed as he jumps, falls, or moves quickly.

Cats have excellent aural abilities and can hear more than a range of ten octaves (two octaves higher than humans), which allows them to hear sounds that we can't. They hear at frequencies of 50 to 65 kilohertz, while humans only can hear 18 to 20 kilohertz. For this reason, many felines are sensitive to noises such as fireworks and loud music.

The Whiskers

A cat's whiskers (also known as *brissae*) are long, stiff hairs that are extremely sensitive to touch.

(If you touch a sleeping cat's whiskers, he will instantly wake up.) Whiskers on the muzzle, the eyebrows, and the elbows act as touch sensors. These sensors are attached to bundles of nerves that can detect the slightest movement. A cat uses his whiskers to navigate around objects in low light. They also allow him to "feel" changes in air currents around objects.

The Eyes

Of all the cat's senses, vision is the most important. His eyes are naturally developed to detect the slightest movement of prey. Cats have superb peripheral vision but are farsighted and cannot focus well on objects that

Cats and kittens come in all shapes, colors, and sizes. The average house cat measures roughly 30 inches (76.2 cm) from nose to tail.

are closer than 2 feet (0.6 m) away. Although cats don't see objects as sharply as humans, being farsighted makes them exceptional hunters.

Because cats are nocturnal, nature also gave them highly effective night vision for hunting. A reflective mirror-like coating, called the *tapetum,* reflects light onto the back of the retina, which helps them to see clearly in near darkness. This reflection of light off the tapetum makes the eyes appear to "glow" in the dark, something you may have noticed in photographs.

Cats and kittens do not see colors like people do, but scientists believe that they can see shades of blue and red.

Cats' eyes are generally one of three shapes—round, almond shaped, or slanted. They have a third eyelid that moves tears across the eye's surface to protect it from injury. This semi-transparent membrane, called a *haw*, occasionally may be seen in the inner corner of the eye. However, the haw should not be visible for long periods of time. If it is exposed on a regular basis, it could be a sign of illness.

The Nose

With about 200 million olfactory cells designed for detecting scents, a cat's sense of smell is 30 times more developed than it is in people. Cats and kittens have a special organ called the *Jacobson's organ* located at the top of the hard palate in their mouth. This organ (also known as the *vomeronasal organ*) analyzes molecules that make up different smells. If a cat sniffs you with his mouth open and looks like

SENIOR CAT TIP

When Cats Are Considered Seniors

Cats are considered "seniors" at about seven or eight years of age. However, each cat ages differently, and based on overall health, environment, and diet, you may not see any signs of aging until your pet is about ten years old. Cats from 10 to 12 years of age are considered geriatric. Due to advances in veterinary care and feline medicine, most indoor cats live 15 to 18 years, and some can live into their 20s.

Aging is controlled by a genetic biological clock in the brain (the hypothalamus), which controls the body's hormones and affects the aging process. As a cat ages, certain metabolic changes occur in the body. Some owners see various outward signs of this gradual process in their pets, such as a general slowing down, lack of interest in play, loss of appetite, and increased sleeping. Changes in the body's functions and metabolism are also occurring, and senior cats may develop digestive, heart, and urinary problems, as well as diabetes and other diseases.

A well-balanced diet, exercise, regular veterinary checkups, and a happy home life will help to keep your senior cat with you for many years to come.

he's sneering at you, he's really just breathing hard to pass scent molecules over the Jacobson's organ. (This process is known as *flehmening*.)

The Teeth

A cat's teeth are designed for tearing, grasping, and shredding prey. Adults have 30 teeth, while kittens have 26 deciduous (baby, or milk) teeth. At around three-and-a-half to four-and-a-half months of age, kittens begin teething. By the time they are six months old, they lose all their baby teeth and grow a full set of adult teeth. Some cats may develop problems with their teeth as they age. Common dental problems for seniors include sensitive teeth, gum disease, loose teeth, and tooth decay.

The Tongue

If a cat has ever licked you, you know that his tongue feels rough, like sandpaper. The tongue is covered with hundreds of *papillae*—tiny backward-facing hook-like structures that act like a natural hairbrush, which a cat uses for grooming the coat.

In the wild, cats use their rough tongues to lick meat off bones. Their taste buds are located on the sides, tip, and back of the tongue.

Cats and kittens can taste bitter, acid, and salty flavors but not sweet tastes. When drinking,

they curl their tongue in at the sides to form a cup or spoon to lap up the liquid.

Coloration

The color or pattern of a cat's coat varies depending on the breed and its heritage. Certain breeds (such as the Siamese) are known for their specific colorings or markings. Nonpurebreds (or moggies) have coats in a variety of different patterns (including blotches, stripes, and solids), as well as in an assortment of colors (such as gray, white, cream, silver, brown, orange, or black). An albino cat's coat completely lacks color pigments, and the eyes are pink. Albinos differ from all-white cats, who have pigmented eyes that may be green, blue, gold, or yellow.

Temperament and Behavior

Cats are mysterious creatures. To people who don't own cats, or to those

No two cats are exactly alike; they each have their own personality quirks and preferences.

who've never tried to understand them, they may appear moody, aloof, and unfriendly. Anyone who has never lived with one may find them perplexing, mischievous, and in some cases, as needy as a small child. But a person who understands cats will quickly tell you that they are warm, affectionate companions with a high intellect and an independent spirit.

Independent Loners?

Cats have a reputation for being antisocial loners, and to some degree, this is true. In the wild, they are solitary hunters who don't seek out other cats for socialization. They live alone, hunt alone, and most of the time prefer to be left alone. (Lions are the exception to this rule; they live in prides and hunt together as a unit.) This sense of independence and self-reliance is one reason why many cat owners prefer cats as pets. Unlike dogs, they don't mind being left alone all day, and they do not need to be let outside to tend to their bathroom needs. However, if cats are left completely alone for long periods of time or become bored with their surroundings, they will find interesting ways to amuse themselves. This is why some cats "act up" or misbehave and do things they shouldn't, like shred toilet paper or explore off-limit areas of your countertop.

Love of People

Despite their independent nature, cats and kittens do love their human companions. Over time, they bond closely to their families, and given the

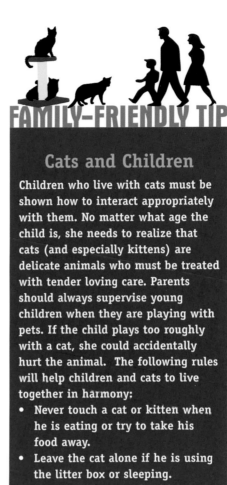

FAMILY-FRIENDLY TIP

Cats and Children

Children who live with cats must be shown how to interact appropriately with them. No matter what age the child is, she needs to realize that cats (and especially kittens) are delicate animals who must be treated with tender loving care. Parents should always supervise young children when they are playing with pets. If the child plays too roughly with a cat, she could accidentally hurt the animal. The following rules will help children and cats to live together in harmony:

- Never touch a cat or kitten when he is eating or try to take his food away.
- Leave the cat alone if he is using the litter box or sleeping.
- Do not pull on a cat's whiskers, ears, tail, or paws.
- Always treat the cat or kitten kindly and gently.

right amount of attention, will often communicate with them. Unlike dogs, cats do not see people as part of their pack or consider their owner to be their "master." If anything, they consider their human to be an equal (or just another big cat).

Despite their independent nature, cats bond closely to their families, and given the right amount of attention, will often communicate with them.

Anyone who owns a cat or kitten must remember that each is a unique individual. No two cats are exactly alike, and they each have their own personality quirks and preferences. Some kittens and cats crave affection and will curl up on your lap at night, while others will be content to sit next to you on the arm of the sofa. Cats and kittens love to play and enjoy interacting with their owners during their daily playtime.

Intelligence

Cats are incredibly intelligent creatures. Their history as wild hunters has taught them how to be self-sufficient. They learn quickly (when they want to) and have good problem-solving skills.

Despite popular belief, cats and kittens can be trained to perform tricks—and they can teach themselves a few tricks, too (such as how to open cabinets, doors, etc.). They can even learn practical "tricks," such as responding to their name, coming when called, and how to walk on a leash. Some owners enjoy spending time teaching their cats to do more complex stunts, such as rolling over, lying down, sitting on command, and jumping through hoops. However, a cat won't learn anything that he doesn't want to. Unlike dogs, cats have no need to impress or please their "masters," but if they see a reward or an advantage to learning something, they will give it a try.

Cat psychology is a mystery to owners and scientists alike. These marvelous creatures always have a reason for doing what they do—even if the reason is "because I feel like it." Cats may ignore things that don't interest them, but they have excellent memories. They remember people who are kind (or unkind) to them, can recall negative situations (such as a trip to the vet's office), and are generally good judges of character. If your cat takes a great dislike to a visiting friend or relative, there's probably a good reason for it.

As pets go, cats and kittens are ideal companions. They adapt quickly to almost any lifestyle and are content to live wherever you do—whether it's in a tiny condo or in a large country home. They often are accepted into apartment complexes and other living situations that do not allow dogs. They are naturally quiet animals (with the exception of the vocal Siamese), and they won't disturb the neighbors by barking as some dogs do.

Cats are also self-reliant. You can leave them home alone for hours while you're at work, and they won't mind. In most cases, a cat will sleep all day while you're gone. When you come home, they will rush to greet you and be ready to play or cuddle. Cats and kittens know how to use the litter box with little or no training, and they are smart enough to learn that certain places in the home are off-limits.

Cats are for cat lovers, and most owners couldn't imagine living without one or more of these intelligent, loving pets.

Be a Responsible Cat Owner

Owning a pet is a lifelong commitment that should not be taken lightly. After all, your cat or kitten is relying on you to provide all of his needs for the rest of his life. Responsibilities of a loving cat owner include the following:

- accepting the financial cost of caring for a kitten or cat (food, supplies, and veterinarian visits can be expensive)
- taking the cat to the veterinarian for regular checkups (not just when he becomes ill)
- keeping the cat safely indoors at all times
- scooping out the litter box, feeding the cat daily, and supplying him with fresh water each day
- playing with the cat and giving him the daily socialization and love that he deserves

Chapter 2

The Stuff of

Everyday Life

Before you bring a cat or kitten home, you need to make preparations for his arrival. Stop at your local pet supply store and purchase all the necessities your kitty will require to settle in comfortably. By planning ahead, you can have everything set up and ready for your new family member so that this transition into an unfamiliar place is a safe and stress-free experience for him.

ake sure that your cat or kitten has had a veterinary checkup and has received all the necessary vaccinations before his arrival or shortly thereafter. This is especially important if you have other pets in the house. While your cat is getting his physical, you can stock up on any additional supplies that the vet may recommend.

Cat Carriers

The first item that you must purchase is a carrier. You will need one in which to bring the cat home and to take him to and from his veterinary checkup. Cardboard carriers or metal cages are not recommended for cats. A determined feline easily can claw his way through the sides of a cardboard enclosure, and they're not very sturdy.

Also, most cats dislike them because they are dark and do not provide enough ventilation. Wire cages are not comfortable for cats to sit in, and they are big and bulky for owners to move.

The ideal cat carrier should be made of sturdy plastic and have a locking, grill-type front door. This will enable the animal to see where he is going, plus it ensures that the enclosure has good airflow. Buy one that has a secure handle and a solid base; it also should be well-designed so that it is easy to maneuver and so that it allows the cat to be placed inside without difficulty. You can put an old towel or sweatshirt on the floor of the enclosure so that your pet has a soft place to sit while traveling.

When choosing an appropriate carrier, consider long-term size

Before you bring your new cat home, you need to make preparations for his arrival by purchasing everything he'll need to settle in comfortably.

requirements. If you're bringing home a tiny kitten, buy a carrier that will be big enough for him when he is full-grown. This will save you money because you won't need to get another carrier when your kitten reaches adulthood. Any enclosure should be large enough for the cat to sit, stand, turn around, and lie down in.

If you are bringing home two kittens (or already have a cat at home), you still need to buy another carrier. As a rule, every cat in the home should have his own.

Litter Boxes

After the cat carrier, the litter box is the next important item on your shopping list. The litter box will be used every day, and it's crucial that your cat takes to it. Each cat in the house should have his own litter box. This prevents territorial squabbling and gives each individual some privacy.

There are many different styles available. If possible, find out what type of box that the cat (or kitten) has been using and buy a similar one. Switching the type of litter box might confuse your cat, which can lead to problems. If you are bringing home a kitten, purchase a litter box specifically designed for kittens. They have low sides and allow the youngsters to climb in and out of the box easily.

SENIOR CAT TIP

Adopting an Older Cat

If you bring home an older cat, he may be afraid of his new surroundings and confused about where he is. Give him quiet time to explore and get comfortable. Don't invite friends and neighbors over to look at him, because this may make him nervous. Show the cat where the litter box, food and water dishes, and scratching post are, and then let him settle in at his own pace. Talk to him in a soothing voice, and give him something to eat. If he seems interested, play with him for a while so that he begins to bond with you.

An older cat has a history that you may not know about. He may have left a loving family or a long-time companion animal behind before he came to live with you, or he could have been mistreated or abandoned. If you happen to know the previous owners, or if you learned about his past when you adopted him, you can make settling in easier. If you know his name, use it often— it will give him a sense of comfort. If you don't, give your cat a chance to get used to his new one.

Some older cats will adapt to a new home right away, while others may hide under the bed for a day or two. Be patient, and give your feline companion plenty of love, praise, and encouragement while he makes the adjustment to living with you.

19

The first item that you must purchase for your cat is a carrier. It should be made of sturdy plastic and have a locking, grill-type front door.

Self-Cleaning Litter Boxes

Self-cleaning (or automated) litter boxes have a sensor attached to a mechanical arm that automatically rakes the litter after the cat has left the box. The arm sweeps the soiled litter and waste to one end where it is collected in a tray. Some cats are scared by them and refuse to use them. These types of litter boxes are often quite expensive.

Hooded Litter Boxes

A hooded (or covered) litter box has a plastic bottom and a tall hood that snaps onto the rim. This design gives the cat privacy while he's using the box and keeps the contents from view. However, some cats do not like the "claustrophobic" feeling that they get while inside of it, and they may

be afraid to use it. Also, hooded boxes can trap odors if there is inadequate ventilation, and they are very dark inside. An advantage to using this type of box is that a cat cannot kick litter (or waste) out of the box and make a mess.

Open-Air Litter Boxes

The most commonly used type of litter box is an open-air box. These boxes have open tops and are about 3 or 4 inches (7.6 or 10.2 cm) high. This item is inexpensive and can be purchased at most grocery stores.

Scoops

After you've found the litter box that you want, you may need to purchase a litter scoop. (Some boxes come with a scoop.) Usually made of plastic, the scoop should have slits in the bottom wide enough for you to sift the litter and remove the waste.

Cat Litter

Pet supply manufacturers have designed many varieties of cat litter, including clay, silica crystals, scented litter, and clumping litter. Before you buy any, find out what type and brand your cat was using and buy a bag of that. Cats become used to the feel and scent of their "regular" litter, and suddenly changing types or brands could cause them to stop using the litter box.

If you decide to change types, do so gradually. Mix some of the new litter in with the old, and over the course of a few weeks, increase the amount of the new type in the box. Your cat will adjust better to the slow change and become accustomed to it.

Whatever type of litter you buy, make sure that it's very absorbent and doesn't give off a lot of dust. Breathing in litter dust is not good for your cat's lungs. Here are a few of the more common types of cat litter available:

- *Clay litter* is inexpensive, and it is the most commonly used litter. It is very absorbent and comes in several varieties, such as dust-free, dust-reduced, scented, and unscented. Some brands are designed for multiple cat households and contain more odor-absorbing materials.
- Litter made of *paper* or *wood pellets* (such as pine) can be expensive, but it does absorb odors effectively. Wood pellets are a good alternative for cats who do not like the feel of clay litter on their feet.
- *Scoopable* (or *clumping*) *clay litter* lasts longer than "regular" or nonclumping litter, but it can be expensive. This litter forms semi-solid clumps when wet. Some cat owners like this type best because it makes cleaning the box easier—you just have to scoop out the clumps. However, it is not recommended for use in homes with kittens. If a kitten walks through a wet patch of litter and then licks his feet, he could ingest the clumping material, which could lead to a serious blockage of the intestinal tract.

- *Crystals* and *"pearls"* are very absorbent and dust-free types of litter. Made from silica gel or sand, crystals and pearls are designed to evaporate moisture and absorb liquid without clumping. Their design makes cleanup easy, but they can be expensive.

Food and Water Dishes

When choosing a set of food and water dishes for your cat, buy something that is sturdy, dishwasher safe, and made of glass or ceramic. If you buy a fancy painted bowl, make sure that it's marked "safe for food." Many decorative bowls contain lead in the paint or glaze, which is poisonous when consumed. As a basic rule, if the food

The litter box will be used every day, so it's crucial that your cat takes to it. Find out the type your cat has been using and buy a similar one.

Set a Schedule

Cats are creatures of habit and often don't like changes or surprises. A stable routine in their lives gives them a sense of comfort and security, a sign that all is well with their world. In fact, once a cat has established a daily routine or pattern, he may become upset, stressed, or confused if the pattern is suddenly altered or disrupted. When you bring your new cat home, set up a daily schedule and stick to it. Develop a routine for exercise/playtime, grooming, feeding, sleeping, and cleaning out the litter box. Follow this pattern at the same time every day. This will build trust and let your cat know what to expect and when.

and water dishes are safe for people to use, then they're safe for your cat.

Although plastic bowls are commonly sold in pet supply stores and are easy to clean, they are not recommended. They tend to get scratched easily and could house bacteria that will make your cat or kitten sick. (Some cats like to play with lightweight plastic bowls by flipping them over and swatting them around the floor for fun.) Stainless steel bowls are not a good choice either. Even though they are dishwasher safe and sturdy, they may give food and water a metallic taste. And if the food doesn't smell and taste good, your cat won't eat it. Whatever type of dishes you purchase, make sure that they are washed out and refilled every day.

Some owners like to purchase automatic watering devices (such as drinking fountains) or self-filling water bowls for their cats. These are hard to tip over, and they ensure that the cat will have access to plenty of water. Remember, though, as with the regular water dish, the self-waterer must be emptied out, cleaned, and refilled with fresh water daily.

Kitten owners should purchase "kitten-sized" food and water bowls. These dishes are smaller and shallower than bowls made for adults. This is important because a small kitten might not be able to reach into the bottom of a large bowl to eat or drink. Kitten-sized dishes can be found in grocery stores and pet supply stores.

If you have more than one cat in your home, make sure that each one has his own set of dishes. This prevents fighting over food and lets you monitor how much each cat consumes.

Cat or Kitten Food

Before you bring home your cat or kitten, find out what kind of food he was eating and buy a bag or box of the same kind. Your new pet may be hungry when he arrives, and the smell and taste of familiar food will comfort him. (For more information on choosing cat food and feeding, see Chapter 3.)

Food and water dishes should be sturdy, dishwasher safe, and made of glass or ceramic.

Scratching Posts

All cats and kittens are compelled to scratch as part of their natural behavior. Scratching is beneficial because it allows them to shed the sheaths of their claws and to stretch. You must provide at least one good-quality scratching post. (If your cat does not have a scratching post to use, he may resort to scratching your furniture or cabinets.) In a multiple cat household, each cat should have his own scratching post.

Multiple Cat Households

If you are a cat lover with a big heart, you may want to adopt every homeless cat in the animal shelter, but be realistic. You cannot take in every stray who comes along. So how many cats are too many? It depends on the size of your home and your budget. Each cat you adopt will need plenty of space in your house, his own litter box, food dishes, and annual veterinary care. Owning 3 cats is realistic, but owning 10 or 15 could quickly become unmanageable. Some cat owners like to start out with a pair of kittens (they can play together and grow up together), while others are content with one cat who becomes a devoted companion. However many cats you adopt, make sure that each one is given lots of love and the best care possible.

Your local pet supply store will have a variety of scratching posts from which to choose. Most are made from wood covered with carpeting. Some are made of sisal string, cardboard, or natural wood. When choosing one, make sure that it has a sturdy, wide base so that your cat cannot knock it over when scratching. The post should be tall enough so that he can stand on his back feet, anchor in his front feet, and claw away.

Place the post near the area in which your cat normally sleeps—they like to stretch and scratch after they wake up from a nap. If you have a large home, you may want to buy a few scratching posts and place them all over the house so that your feline companion always has one nearby.

Keep an eye on the condition of the scratching post. If it becomes worn out or frayed, replace it with a new one.

Kitty Condos

A trip to the pet store will give you many ideas about the types, sizes, and styles of cat condos or perches available. Some condos are designed like playgrounds, with perches, ledges, hideaways, and toys to keep your cat entertained. Depending on your budget, you can buy carpeted condos that double as hideaways and scratching posts or towers with several levels that allow your cat to sit up high and survey his domain.

Beds

Cats sleep about 60 percent of their lives, and they are known to nap anywhere that is comfortable. Even though some make their own beds (on a guest bed, blanket, or in your closet), you should buy your cat a bed of his own. It will give him a familiar, safe place to sleep that belongs only to him.

Pet supply stores sell many different types. Most are lined with cotton, flannel, or sheepskin. The one that you buy should be large enough for your cat to curl up in, but it shouldn't be huge. Cats need to feel secure wherever they sleep, and touching the sides of their bed gives them a sense of security. Put it in an area where your cat is not likely to be disturbed by loud noises or people wandering in and out. Before you know it, he will snuggle right in.

Collars

Every pet should wear a collar with identification at all times. Your cat's collar should be made of stretchable nylon or have an automatic release or safety clasp that will engage if he gets caught on something, like a fence post or a tree branch. Pet supply manufacturers design fancy collars in many styles, colors, and designs, but whatever type you buy, make sure that you get the right size for your pet. Collars come in a variety of sizes based on the size and weight of the cat. For

Indoors or Outdoors?

Should you allow your cat to go outside, or should you keep him as an "indoor-only" pet? This is a topic that many owners disagree about. Some cat lovers insist on keeping their cats inside all the time, while others feel that they're depriving their pets of the "fun" of roaming free after being trapped inside the house all day.

The major advantage to keeping your cat indoors is safety. Cats who wander outdoors often get into serious trouble or may even be killed. If your pet is roaming on his own, you have no control over whom or what he encounters. The outside world is a big place with many hazards, and your cat could run into trouble.

An "indoor-only" cat will not have to face the dangers of the outside world, such as poisonous fertilizers and pesticides, antifreeze, motor vehicles, threatening people (who could steal or injure him), dogs, wild animals (such as skunks, raccoons, snakes, bees, and wasps), weather hazards (frostbite or heatstroke), and even other cats.

A cat who is allowed to stray can come into contact with another sick cat (or other animal) and pick up parasites (such as fleas and ticks) or diseases (such as feline leukemia or rabies.) If an outdoor cat isn't spayed or neutered, he or she will likely contribute to the cat overpopulation problem.

Cats who are kept indoors don't have to worry about any of these hazards. As a result of their safe, controlled living conditions, they live much longer. As a responsible owner, you owe it to your pet to do what's best for him, and the best way to know that your cat is safe is to keep him inside.

example, if you have a kitten, he should wear a "kitten-sized" collar. Keep in mind that as your kitten grows up, he will need a larger collar.

The collar should be loose enough around your cat's neck so he can breathe and swallow normally, but it shouldn't be so loose that he can pull it off or get his foot trapped in it. As a rule, leave enough space to slip two fingers between the neck and the collar. If your cat has never worn a collar before, he will probably not like the feel of it around his neck and will likely try to pull it off. This is normal cat behavior. After a few days, he will get used to it and forget that he's wearing it.

Leashes and Harnesses

Some owners like to train their cats to walk on a leash. If you decide to take your feline friend outdoors for a walk,

you'll need to buy a harness and leash. The leash should be no longer than 3 feet (0.9 m) in length. This will allow you to keep him close to you as you walk.

There are many different styles of harnesses available, but no matter what type you choose, it must be escape-proof and fit securely around your cat so that he cannot wriggle free. Harnesses are sold based on the size and weight of the cat. The one you choose should fit snugly around the body, but it shouldn't be so tight that you cannot slip two fingers between the harness and the cat.

Before you go outside, let your feline companion become used to the feel of the harness around his body. Practice walking him on the leash and harness indoors for a few days or until he is comfortable wearing it. If he becomes upset, take it off and try again later.

ID Tags and Microchips

ID tags could save your cat's life. If he gets lost, the collar and tag will let someone know where he belongs. (Most pets who have IDs find their way home after a brief separation.) The ID tag should have your name and phone number on it, along with your cat's name. You can order them from pet supply catalogs or from pet supply sites on the Internet. Some pet supply stores and department stores have automated machines that make engraved ID tags in a few minutes.

Instead of relying on metal ID tags, some owners use microchips to identify their pets. A veterinarian can inject a microchip directly into your cat or kitten. The chip doesn't harm him, and it can be inserted at about eight weeks of age. It is a permanent form of identification, and it cannot become lost or removed by the cat because it is placed under the muscle near the shoulder. If your pet gets lost and is turned into an animal rescue organization or shelter, the workers will scan him and use the special code on the chip to contact you. Whether you opt for microchipping or the more traditional metal ID tags, remember to update your contact information if you move.

Grooming Supplies

Although cats are very clean animals who groom themselves every day, they need some grooming assistance from time to time. When buying your pet supplies, purchase a brush and comb designed for cats. If you have a long-haired cat (such as a Persian), you need to buy a brush and comb designed for grooming long-haired breeds. Smaller, softer brushes and combs are also available for kittens.

Other grooming supplies you should have on hand include cotton balls, mineral oil, a small pair of scissors, pet shampoo, a towel, a toothbrush designed for cats, feline-safe toothpaste,

FAMILY-FRIENDLY TIP

Young Helpers

If you have a child in the family, she may want to take care of the new cat or kitten. While you should encourage children to help out with daily care, they should never be solely responsible for a pet's well-being. Even if they promise to "always" take responsibility, they often become bored with daily chores and may forget to change the cat's water or to provide food every day. This is unfair to the animal and does not promote responsible pet ownership.

However, you can teach your child by example—by allowing her to help you. Depending on the child's age, she can do simple chores (such as change the cat's water), but until she reaches an appropriate age and maturity level, the cat's needs must be tended to by an adult.

27

nail clippers made for cats, and a styptic pencil. (Grooming basics will be discussed in Chapter 4.)

Cat Toys

Every cat needs to have a set of toys. Cats and kittens are very inventive and have been known to entertain themselves with items found around the home. There are many types of pet toys available, so you're guaranteed to find several that your cat will love. Depending on your budget, you can buy mechanical or battery-operated toy mice or birds, or simple low-cost toys like a catnip mouse.

Before you buy any toy, be sure that it's safe for your cat. Examine all toys before you bring them home, and make sure that they do not have any small pieces that could fall off or be clawed off or chewed off, because they could become a choking hazard. Avoid toys with small parts like bells, glued-on plastic eyes, pompoms, small foam balls (your cat can chew off the foam and swallow it), marbles, feathers, or anything small enough to go down your cat's throat. Never let him play in or around a plastic bag—it is not a toy. The bag's handles could slip over your cat's head or wrap around his throat, and he could suffocate. Safe choices include ping-pong balls, small plastic balls, paper bags (with no handles), cardboard boxes, balls of paper, rolled-up socks, and catnip mice.

Rotate the toys every few weeks to keep your cat interested. If you discover that a toy is worn or cracked, replace it with a new one. Leave the toys out while you're at work or gone for the day so that your cat can play when you're not home. They will help to keep him from becoming bored.

Sharing your home with a cat or kitten can be a rewarding experience. You'll take on new responsibilities, have new challenges, and become an important part of your cat's daily life. In return, your feline companion will give you enjoyment, loving affection, and brighten your days for many years to come.

Common Household Dangers

It's important that you safeguard your home (or "cat-proof" it) before your new cat arrives. Cats and kittens are very curious, and they will find hazards that you never even knew existed. If you've never owned a cat before, get down on your hands and knees and look around from your cat's point of view. You'll be amazed at what you find.

There are many household items we take for granted and use in our everyday lives that can be poisonous or otherwise dangerous to your pet. Some of these include:

- household hazards (such as unsecured doors and window screens, lit stoves, ovens, dryers, electric appliances, electrical cords, recliners, and swivel chairs)
- choking hazards (small objects that are easily swallowed include: paper clips, pen tops, rubber bands, thumbtacks, buttons, bones, coins, dental floss, nails, screws, and staples)
- toxic plants (some common toxic plants include: aloe vera, baby's breath, daffodil, Easter lily, eucalyptus, geranium, holly, iris, marigold, mistletoe, morning glory, peony, philodendron, poinsettia, primrose, tiger lily, tulip), dried floral arrangements (they may contain chemical preservatives that are poisonous)
- cleaners such as laundry detergent, bleach, and drain cleaner
- insecticides and fertilizers
- antifreeze, gasoline, paint thinner, and mothballs
- drugs and medications (including acetaminophen, ibuprofen, and aspirin)
- alcohol
- holiday hazards (including lit candles, glass ornaments, tinsel, ribbons, bows, metal hooks, and chocolate)

Keep all hazardous materials away from your cat. Be sure to teach your family members about cat-proofing your house and the importance of feline safety. Go to the ASPCA's website at www.aspca.org for more information on pet safety.

Chapter 3

Good Eating

As your cat's caretaker, you are responsible for providing him with a balanced diet of good-quality food. This means making sure that he eats the best food possible and receives all the vitamins and minerals necessary to live a long and healthy life.

Food Basics

Cats are carnivores, and they require a diet that primarily consists of meat. Left to fend for themselves, cats in the wild will catch a bird or a mouse and consume almost all of it—including the bones, feathers or fur, internal organs, and muscle meat. The meat and internal organs provide essential proteins, vitamins, and minerals, while the bones and/or feathers are a source of fiber. The prey's stomach contents provide the small amount of vegetable matter that cats need.

Pet food manufacturers have studied the exact nutritional requirements that felines require to maintain good health. A high-quality food containing the right amounts of proteins, fats, vitamins, and minerals will supply your cat with a daily balanced diet.

To keep your cat at optimum health, feed him a balanced daily diet of good-quality food.

32

Proteins

A cat's diet should consist of approximately 30 to 35 percent muscle meat. Meat contains proteins, enzymes, and amino acids that are essential to the body. Protein is the body's basic building material and helps to repair body tissue, aids in growth, and helps to regulate the metabolism.

Taurine is an amino acid that is essential for the health of all cats and kittens. A taurine-deficient diet could produce heart disease, nervous system disorders, stunted growth, eye problems, and in severe cases, blindness or death. Kittens require more taurine than adults, and "kitten formula" food contains the proper amount of this amino acid. Make sure that it is listed as an ingredient in whatever type or brand of food that you feed your cat or kitten. *Never* feed your feline dog food. It doesn't contain taurine, and it is not nutritionally complete for cats.

Carbohydrates and Fats

Carbohydrates should make up approximately 30 percent of a cat's diet. They give the body fuel for energy and add fiber to the diet. Approximately 8 to 10 percent of a cat's diet should come from fats. If fats are lacking in the foods consumed, kittens will have a poor growth rate and the skin and coat will have a dry, dull appearance.

Vitamins and Minerals

Vitamins A, C, and E are called antioxidants. They help to strengthen the immune system and may reduce a cat's risk of developing certain cancers. Unlike humans, cats are able to produce their own vitamin C, so it is not a necessary additive to their food. Vitamin A helps to maintain good vision and skin tone. Vitamin E helps muscle, cell membranc, and organ functions, while vitamin D is essential for healthy bones, teeth, and muscle tone.

B vitamins are important for a healthy coat, skin, and overall growth. They protect the nervous system and aid in the body's metabolic functions. Biotin aids in skin repair, cellular growth, muscle formation, and helps digestion. Niacin is obtained from animal sources and is found in meat and liver; it helps a cat's body utilize energy. Omega-3 and omega-6 fatty acids help to improve the skin and give the coat a healthy, glossy shine.

A high-quality commercially prepared cat or kitten food will provide all the necessary vitamins, minerals, and other nutrients that your cat needs.

Feeding Your Cat

There are many different types of pet food on the market. New cat owners may be overwhelmed when it comes to choosing the "right" type. The most important factor to keep in mind when making a choice is that the food is a good-quality brand and contains all the necessary nutrients.

Kittens and adult cats have different feeding requirements, so it's important that you provide your pet with a balanced and healthy diet for his life stage. Growing kittens need two to three times more calories than adult and

Kittens and adult cats have different feeding requirements, so it's important that you provide your pet with a healthy diet suitable for his life stage.

senior cats. They also need more fats, proteins, vitamins, and taurine in their diet. The best way to ensure that your kitten is receiving the proper amount of nutrients is to feed him food especially designed for him. "Kitten formula" should be clearly marked to indicate that it is 100-percent nutritionally complete and balanced for growing kittens. They should be fed this formula until they reach one year of age.

Adult cats don't need the high-calorie food that kittens do, and feeding them this food will make them fat. In addition to the "regular" types of cat food on the market, there are many specialty formulas available for adults. Pet food manufacturers have created specialty foods for dental care, hairball control, senior cats, overweight cats, cats with urinary tract problems, and even indoor cats.

Types of Cat Food

Commercially Prepared Foods

Commercially prepared foods (found in grocery stores and pet supply stores) are the most common types fed to cats and kittens. A high-quality commercially prepared food contains the proper amounts of proteins, vitamins, minerals, and other ingredients that are needed to maintain good health.

Be aware, however, that not all commercially prepared foods are created equal. Supermarket or generic brands are inexpensive, but they may contain high amounts of sugar, preservatives, salt, artificial colorings and flavorings, and meat by-products. Some are low quality and may not be 100-percent nutritionally complete or balanced for your cat.

Changing Food

If you change brands or flavors of cat food, do it gradually. Cats are very sensitive to change—especially when it comes to their food—and if you suddenly change their diet, they may refuse the new food or develop stomach upset. To compromise with your cat and get him accustomed to his new food, slowly incorporate it into his regular brand. Each time you feed him, increase the percentage of the new brand while decreasing the percentage of the regular food. Here's how:
• On days 1 and 2, mix 3/4 of the regular food with 1/4 of the new food.
• On days 3 and 4, make a 50/50 blend of regular food and new food.
• For the next 3 days, mix 3/4 of the new food with 1/4 of the old brand of food.
• From then on, serve only the new brand of food.
This gradual change will allow your cat to adjust to the diet change comfortably. If he is resistant, slow the change by increasing the time between each step. Depending on the cat, this process could take from 7 to 14 days.

A high-quality cat food contains the proper amounts of proteins, vitamins, minerals, and other ingredients necessary to maintain good health.

National or name brands are medium-priced foods produced by big name manufacturers, and they are especially designed to provide a 100-percent nutritionally complete diet. These products contain all the ingredients that your cat needs to stay healthy, but many contain meat or animal by-products and not quality meat.

Meat or animal by-products are not muscle meat—they are leftover parts of an animal that are not fit to be fed to people. By-products include internal organs, skin, feathers, beaks, bones, and other parts of the animal. Many cat owners refuse to feed their pets anything containing these by-products because they're not sure exactly what they're feeding. Others see nothing wrong with feeding by-products and argue that in the wild, cats consume many of the same ingredients (such as internal organs and skin).

Premium brands are usually more expensive than other brands, but they are made with superior ingredients. They generally contain little or no added preservatives, colorings, or flavorings and are made with meat, not meat by-products. These foods can be purchased from most veterinarians or pet supply stores.

Varieties

Commercially prepared cat food comes in three varieties—canned (or wet), dry, and semi-moist. Many owners feed a combination of canned food and dry food. Offer your cat some of each and see if he has a preference.

CANNED FOOD

Canned cat food is generally more expensive than the dry or semi-moist variety. It is 50 to 78 percent water and can be fed alone or as a supplement to dry food. When buying canned food, avoid buying a brand that contains a lot of added preservatives (the canning process preserves the can's contents, so there is no need for preservatives),

and avoid brands listing meat or animal by-products as the main ingredient. It's also a good idea to check the can for a freshness date or expiration date.

Canned food has less preservatives and additives than dry or semi-moist food, and it is the healthiest option for your cat or kitten. However, it cannot be left out in the dish all day. Dispose of uneaten food after 20 minutes, and cover and refrigerate any unused portion.

DRY FOOD

When buying dry food, make sure that the first ingredient is meat, not meat by-products, cornmeal, or any other type of grain or meal. Check the bag or box for an expiration date. Although dry food has a long shelf life, it will become stale if the bag is left open or if it is not used quickly. Store dry food in an airtight plastic container, and don't buy more than your cat or kitten will eat in a month.

One benefit to feeding dry food is that you can leave the food out all day (for free feeding) and it will not spoil. Some seniors may have a hard time chewing dry food, so if your senior cat is missing teeth or has sensitive teeth, you may want to give him canned food or a blend of dry and canned food.

SEMI-MOIST FOOD

Semi-moist cat food generally is not recommended as a main food for your pet. High amounts of preservatives are added to it to keep it moist and increase its shelf life. It contains high amounts of chemicals, artificial flavorings, colorings, and sugar.

Reading Labels

No matter what brand of food you buy, always read the list of ingredients on the box, bag, or can. A cat food labeled with the words "meets the nutritional levels for a complete diet" or "provides complete and balanced nutrition as established by the Association of American Feed Control Officials (AAFCO)" means that the food provides all the necessary proteins, fats, nutrients, vitamins, and minerals. Avoid buying cat (or kitten) food that does not state this on the label or packaging. Always buy food that is appropriate to the life stage of your pet. If you're buying food specifically for kittens, the label should state somewhere that the food is nutritionally balanced and appropriate for their changing needs.

Commercially prepared food comes in canned, moist, and dry varieties, so try offering your cat some of each to see if he has a preference.

37

Good Eating

expensive than other "traditional" types of cat food, but if you follow an organic diet for yourself, you may decide to do the same for your cat.

Nontraditional Diets

Some owners prefer to make their cats' meals. This way, they can control exactly what goes into their pets' food, and they know and trust what they are consuming. The ingredients are often natural and fresh, and depending on the food that you prepare for your cat, you can choose a nonorganic or organic home-cooked diet, or a raw diet.

Home-Cooked Diets

Providing your cat with a home-cooked diet is a lot of work. The meat, vegetables, and other ingredients need to be lightly cooked and served to your cat warm. (Food smells and tastes better to cats if it's at room temperature.) If you decide to provide a home-cooked diet, you'll have to prepare batches of food every day or plan ahead and make enough to last for a few days by freezing the leftover portions. This means that you'll be

Some sensitive cats have had allergic reactions to the chemicals and other ingredients found in this type of food.

Organic Cat Food

Organic cat and kitten food comes in several varieties and can be found in health food stores and pet supply stores. Organic foods contain ingredients that are grown or raised without pesticides, chemical fertilizers, growth hormones, or antibiotics. There are no preservatives, chemical flavorings, colorings, or other additives, so it does not have a long shelf life. It is also more

SENIOR CAT TIP

Feeding Older Cats

Because of their advanced age, senior and geriatric cats should be given special feeding considerations. Older cats can develop tooth problems and may find it hard to eat dry food. If that's the case with your senior cat, switch his diet to canned food or moisten the dry food with some canned food.

A cat's metabolism slows as he ages, and his senses of smell and taste begin to diminish. As a result, many older cats lose interest in food and become too thin. If your senior cat seems to have lost his appetite, try offering him some dry food soaked in warm chicken or beef broth. You also can switch to a canned-food-only diet. Canned food tastes and smells more appealing than dry food, and it's easier to digest.

When cats age, they slow down and become less active. As a result, senior or geriatric cats require fewer calories than middle-aged adult cats do. They need less protein in their diets than active adults. (Too much protein can lead to kidney problems.) Some owners give their older cats a specially formulated food designed for seniors. Ask your veterinarian if your cat needs a special diet or any vitamin supplements to keep him healthy and happy in his golden years.

spending a lot of time cooking for your cat, freezing the extra meals, and reheating them.

If you make batches of food ahead of time and freeze the leftovers to use later, don't defrost them in the microwave. Microwave ovens destroy essential enzymes and drain food of vitamins. Instead, leave the prepared food in the refrigerator to thaw slowly, or place the bag or container in a pot of hot water to thaw.

What kind of food goes into a home-cooked or homemade diet? Practically anything humans would eat. The home-cooked diet is basically a blend of meat, carbohydrates, fats, and vegetables. Some common ingredients include cooked chicken livers, gizzards, hearts, cooked ground beef, duck, venison, lamb, fish, turkey, sardines, cottage cheese, cooked eggs, carrots, broccoli, and other vegetables. If you're making homemade meals for your cat, you can also add baby food (meat or vegetables) into the mix.

Preparing meals for your feline friend can be a very expensive and time-consuming process. If you want to feed a home-cooked diet, talk to your veterinarian first. She will be able to educate you on nutritional requirements and can give you a few basic recipes to follow. Some cats with diseases or allergies have seen improved health conditions when switched to a home-cooked diet. If you have a pet with a chronic illness or disease, ask your veterinarian if this diet could benefit him.

If you like cooking for your cat, there are many websites and books devoted to the subject, and many include recipes. However, always show your veterinarian any recipe you're going to use before you start feeding it to your cat—it never hurts to get a professional opinion.

Raw Food Diets

A raw food diet differs from a home-cooked diet in that the food is given to the cat raw. Advocates of a raw, or natural, diet argue that cooked or processed food isn't natural for cats (after all, nature doesn't cook for cats), and the cooking process destroys necessary enzymes and vitamins in the food.

Because cats have stronger stomach acids than humans do, they are better able to digest raw (or natural) foods. Although it may be hard to convert a cat who is used to a traditional commercial food diet, cats usually can live well on a raw diet. If you are feeding your feline a raw diet, use caution when handling raw meat to avoid exposing yourself to *E. coli* and other bacteria that may be present in raw foods. Consult your veterinarian for advice and recipes before offering this diet.

If you feed your cat a home-cooked or raw diet and go away on vacation, you'll have to leave prepared food for him and show the person who's taking care of your pet exactly how to prepare the meals.

Some cats with diseases or allergies have seen improved health conditions when switched to a home-cooked diet.

Homemade Meals and Supplements

If you're feeding your cat or kitten a home-cooked diet, you need to add vitamin supplements to the food. You can purchase feline vitamin supplements from a veterinarian or at a pet supply store. These vitamins come either in a tablet form that can be crushed up and mixed with the food or in a liquid that can be given directly or added to the food.

If you give your cat or kitten a 100-percent balanced commercially prepared food, no supplements are needed. Adding extra vitamins to your cat's diet can be dangerous, so do not add them unless your veterinarian specifically instructs you to do so. The vet will tell you what type, dosage, and frequency of supplementation that your pet needs (if any).

Water

All cats and kittens must have access to fresh, clean water at all times. If you live in an area where the water is treated or has a high sulfur content, you may want to give your cat bottled water or filtered tap water. Cats have keen senses of smell and taste, and they may refuse to drink water that smells bad or tastes like chemicals.

Make sure to replace the water and wash the water dish every day. (After all, your cat can't do it for himself.) Depending on your cat's eating habits, you may have to refill the dish several times a day. Some cats drop food bits into it, play with it and knock it over, or shed hairs into it. If this happens, you need to change the water again. A cat will not drink out of a dirty water dish.

Don't panic if your cat or kitten doesn't look like he is drinking much water. Cats obtain most of the moisture that they require through the food that they eat, and they need less water than most other mammals. Canned food is about 78 percent water, semi-moist food is approximately 35 percent water, and dry food ranges from 6 to 10 percent water, depending on the brand.

No matter what type of food that you feed, your cat or kitten always must have clean water available. (Cats can become constipated if they do not get enough water.) Offering him a bowl of milk is not a substitute for water. Despite the myth, many cats are lactose intolerant.

Feeding Schedule

There are two feeding options available to cat owners—free feeding (also known as self-feeding) and scheduled feeding. You can allow your cat or kitten to self-feed by leaving a portion of dry food out all day. Your feline will be able to eat or snack whenever he wants. This is a good option for people who are at work during the day or for those who work odd hours. However, this type of feeding could lead to weight gain. If your cat eats all day because he is bored or lonely, he may become overweight.

Cats and kittens must have access to fresh, clean water at all times.

end of the day, they offer a scheduled feeding portion. This sets up a routine for the cat and allows him to snack if he becomes hungry when his owner isn't at home.

If you practice scheduled feedings and go away for a weekend trip or a vacation, someone will have to come to your house and feed your cat at the scheduled feeding times. A cat who free feeds on dry food may be left enough food for an overnight trip or a weekend.

If you feed canned food, you'll have to set up a regular feeding schedule so that it does not spoil. You can feed your cat according to your own schedule, such as before you go to work or when you come home in the evening. Keep in mind, however, that once you set this schedule, you must stick to it. Your pet will rely on you for a regular feeding time. Kittens need to eat often, so if you use scheduled feedings for a kitten, you will have to give him food several times a day.

Some owners do a combination of free feeding and scheduled feeding. Before they leave for work, they put out a small portion of dry food for daytime consumption, and when they return home at the

Obesity

Did you know that approximately 25 to 50 percent of cats in the United States are overweight, and another 5 to 15 percent are obese? Depending on gender,

Your cat will rely on you for a regular feeding time; once you set a schedule you must stick to it.

body type, and breed, the average cat should weigh between 9 and 12 pounds (4.1-5.4 kg). Cats are considered overweight when they are 10 percent over their ideal body weight, and they are considered obese when they are 20 percent over their ideal weight.

Obesity in cats is a big problem because most people overfeed them, which leads to weight gain. Cats are small animals, and most only need between 1/4 cup (113 g) and 1/2 cup (227g) of food twice a day. (A cat's stomach is about the size of a 50-cent piece before it expands.) Obesity can lead to health problems, including feline diabetes, heart disease, arthritis, and joint pain.

To determine if your cat is overweight, run your hands along his ribs. You should be able to feel his ribs but not see them. If you feel a thick layer of fat, your cat is overweight and should be put on a diet.

If you have an obese cat, you can help him to lose weight naturally. One way is to reduce the portion sizes of the food that you're feeding. Don't starve your cat or stop regular feedings; simply reduce the amount of food that he gets per serving. A veterinarian can recommend a good-quality diet or weight-maintaining cat food.

Another way to help your cat to lose weight is to increase the amount of exercise

The amount you should feed your cat depends on his size, weight, age, and activity level.

that he gets every day. Schedule small blocks of time (five to ten minutes) each day to play with him. (It can be a simple game of chasing a string, running after a ping-pong ball, or batting a crumpled piece of paper around the house.) Start with short exercise sessions and gradually build on them as your cat's endurance increases. If he likes walking on a leash, take him for a short walk (up and down the driveway) once or twice a day to get him active. Remember, the more your cat moves, the more calories he will burn.

How Much Should You Feed Your Cat?

How much you should feed your cat or kitten is a very subjective topic, and there is no universal answer. The amount of food that a cat or kitten needs depends on his size, weight, age, and activity level. Cats who are allowed to go outside or who exercise a lot will burn more calories and may eat more than a sedentary animal who sleeps all day. Remember that no two cats are alike, even when it comes to food.

All cats and kittens have different appetites, so feeding amounts vary. In general, an adult female requires approximately 200 to 300 calories a day. An average male needs between 250 and 300 calories daily. Adult formula dry cat food contains approximately 400 calories per cup, and canned food contains about 150 calories per cup. (The actual calorie count varies depending on the brand of food.) The

average cat needs approximately 8 ounces (227 g) of food a day.

Kittens grow fast, so they need about two to three times as much food as

FAMILY-FRIENDLY TIP

Kids Can Help With Feeding

Having your child help you to feed the cat is a great way for the child and cat to bond with each other. Depending on the age of the child, she can be given different responsibilities when it comes to feeding time. Younger children can get the food dishes out, choose a can of food, or refill the water bowl each day. Older children can feed the cat, either scooping out the correct portion or giving him the bowl at the appropriately scheduled time each day.

When feeding the cat, explain to your child how much food he needs and how often. You can even have her draw up a feeding chart or schedule that shows when it's feeding time. Always supervise your child when she is feeding a pet, and remember to teach her that the cat shouldn't be disturbed when he's eating. Allowing your child to feed a pet and learn how to take care of him properly teaches responsible pet ownership from an early age.

an adult, and they require small meals several times a day. They should be fed food (wet or dry) specifically designed for kittens until they reach one year of age because they need more proteins, fats, and calories than adults. These formulas are designed to promote healthy growth and development. If a kitten is not given the right amount of nutrients or is otherwise poorly fed, he can develop muscle problems, immune disorders, vision problems, and suffer retarded growth. An adolescent cat (from six months to one year) may look like an adult, but he's still growing and requires extra calories and nutrients as well.

Seniors are generally less active than adults and should be given several small meals throughout the day. Some older cats will not have much of an appetite, so you should offer an appropriate food three to four times a day and adjust the feeding schedules/amounts according to what he eats.

Pet food manufacturers list their recommended feeding portions on the packaging. Follow their guidelines to determine the proper amount to feed. Do some experimentation and adjust the portion to your pet's specific needs. For example, if your cat (or kitten) self-feeds, offer the recommended amount of food and watch to see how long it takes him to finish what you've offered. If he eats everything in the bowl right away, consider increasing the portion. Pet food manufacturers recommend feeding an adult cat approximately 1/2 to 1 cup (227 - 454 g) of dry food a day.

If you're feeding canned food, give your cat the recommended portion and see how much he finishes. If he leaves the bowl half full, cut back on the portion that you're offering. If he eats it all and then begs for more, increase the portion size. Pet food manufacturers recommend feeding an adult cat or a kitten approximately one can of food portioned for two meals a day.

Unlike dogs, cats will stop eating when they are full, so always adjust the portions according to your cat's size and activity level. You are the best judge of his appetite, so use the portion and feeding schedule that best suits his needs.

Feeding Chart

This is an approximate feeding chart based on commercially prepared food. (The amount of a home-cooked diet required by cats and kittens in each stage of life will vary based on the recipe.) For best feeding results, use the manufacturer's recommended feeding instructions as a guide, and then adjust your cat's (or kitten's) portions and feedings according to his specific needs.

Providing your cat or kitten with a nutritionally complete diet is the best way to keep him happy and healthy throughout his lifetime. Offer him the highest quality food that you can afford. Your cat will thank you by looking and feeling better, and he will be with you for many more years to come.

Age	Meals per Day	Type and Amount to Feed	Best Food
Kittens 3 to 6 weeks	5	Dry: 1/4 to 1/3 cup Canned: 1 oz at each feeding	Kitten formula
Kittens 7 weeks to 6 months	4	Dry: 1/3 to 3/4 cup Canned: 1 to 3 oz at each feeding	Kitten formula
Adolescents 6 months to 1 year	3, then gradually reduce to 2	Dry: 1/2 to 1 cup Canned: 2 to 3 oz (adjust as necessary)	Kitten formula
Adults 1 to 7 years	2	Dry: 1/2 to 1 cup Canned: 5 oz (adjust as necessary)	Adult formula
Seniors (starting at 7 to 8 years)	3 to 4 (adjust as necessary)	Dry: 1/2 to 3/4 cup Canned: 3 to 5 oz (adjust as necessary)	Senior formula
Geriatric (10 to 12 years and older)	1 to 2 (adjust as necessary)	Dry: 1/2 to 3/4 cup Canned: 3 to 5 oz (adjust as necessary)	Senior or advanced formula

Chapter 4

Looking Good

Grooming is a great way to keep your feline companion healthy and looking good. Although cats groom themselves daily, your cat or kitten will need your help with some basic tasks. With a few supplies on hand, you can groom your cat at home in just minutes a day.

Coat and Skin Care

It's a good idea to begin a regular grooming schedule when you first bring your cat or kitten home. The sooner you start, the more readily your cat will become used to it. In time, he will accept the grooming procedure as part of his everyday life. If you've adopted an adult cat, be gentle and patient when you begin. He may not have been groomed before or may have been groomed only occasionally, so he may not like being fussed over.

Brushing

Brushing and combing your cat or kitten is a very important part of grooming. Cats (especially long-haired breeds) have a lot of hair. As new hairs grow in, the old hairs are lost, or shed. Fur is shed every day, but excessive shedding is a sign of a medical or emotional condition. Cats who are stressed may overgroom themselves or pull out chunks of their own fur. A nutritional deficiency, parasites, or ringworm also could cause abnormal shedding. If your cat is shedding a lot or pulling out his fur, take him to the vet for a checkup.

Set up a regular brushing routine and stick to it. How often you'll need to brush or comb your cat or kitten depends on his hair length and coat. If you have a long-haired cat with a thick coat (such as a Maine Coon), then you'll have to brush him every day. Short-haired breeds (such as the Burmese) may need only twice-weekly brushing.

Brushing and combing is beneficial because it cuts down on the amount of hair that your cat consumes when he washes himself. A cat who swallows too much loose fur could develop hairballs, constipation, or intestinal blockages. If you see your cat vomiting up extra hair, don't panic. This is a normal reaction. It's nature's way of helping him

Long-Haired vs. Short-Haired Cats

The length of your cat's hair will determine how often you need to groom him. Long-haired breeds (such as the Maine Coon, Persian, and Ragdoll) tend to shed more, so they require daily grooming. Their long hair can become tangled, knotted, or matted if left ungroomed. A cat will groom himself, but the length and amount of hair can be overwhelming for him to do a great job. If you own a long-haired cat, be sure to buy a brush and comb designed for long-haired breeds. You might also consider purchasing a special "hairball prevention" formula dry cat food. This high-fiber food helps extra fur to pass through the digestive system.

Owners of short-haired breeds (including the Siamese, Burmese, and Ocecat) only may need to brush their cat once a week. Although these cats shed just like their long-haired cousins, their fur tends to be less dense, shorter, and in some cases, thinner. Short-haired cats and kittens are less likely to develop hairballs or get their fur tangled or matted.

to expel the extra fur that he's swallowed while bathing.

How to Brush a Cat

Before you begin brushing your cat, first examine the coat for any tangles, knots, or matted fur. (These are common in long-haired breeds.) If you find mats or clumps, don't pull them out. Instead, work the tangled hair apart with your fingers or the comb. If the mat is hopelessly snarled and you cannot get it free, carefully cut it out with scissors. Owners of long-haired breeds should check for mats between the toes, in the ears (especially if your cat has "ear curls"), and around the legs and anus.

Next, begin brushing your cat's head. Use soft, gentle strokes in the direction in which the fur lies as you work your way down the body, sides, and legs. Cats have sensitive skin, so don't brush hard. If you don't feel that you're getting all

the hair off, you can come back and do a second (or even a third) brushing until you get all the loose fur. Remove the hair from the brush whenever it gets full so that you don't put the loose fur back on the cat.

Many felines like the feel of the brush stroking their fur and will welcome a long brushing session. Some may lie down and roll over so that you can brush their stomachs. However, others hate having their legs, feet, or stomachs brushed and may resist or swat at the brush. If this happens, give your cat a minute to settle down, and then try again.

You can brush a cat almost anywhere. Some owners prefer to hold their cat on their lap or sit him on a chair, while others let the cat lie on the floor so that he can stretch out. The choice is yours—and your cat's.

Bathing

Your cat's hair length and coat type will determine how often you need to groom him.

Even though cats wash themselves several times over the course of a day, there could come a time when your cat needs a "real" bath. If you allow him to go outdoors, you may have to give him a scrub from time to time. As a general rule, don't bathe your cat unless he needs it for a specific reason (such as if he gets mud caked in his fur, gets into something sticky, or if he's a show cat and needs to look fantastic for the competition). Overbathing can strip the fur of its natural oils, which results in dry skin and a dull, brittle coat.

Grooming Supplies

Before you can begin grooming your cat or kitten, you need to purchase the following grooming supplies:

- a brush and comb designed for your cat's coat type (long-haired or short-haired)
- a kitten or cat toothbrush (or finger cap)
- feline-safe toothpaste
- a small pair of scissors
- a thick towel
- baby oil or mineral oil
- cotton balls/gauze
- pet shampoo designed for cats and kittens
- special nail clippers designed for use on cats (optional)
- styptic pencil (optional)

When bathing your cat, only use a shampoo that is specifically made for kittens or cats. Shampoos and soaps designed for humans, dogs, or small animals, dishwashing detergent, and dish soap contain harsh chemicals that could make your cat sick.

How to Bathe a Cat

Most cats don't like to get wet and will resist taking a bath, but if you need to bathe your cat, here's how:

- Put a nonskid mat, towel, or bath mat in the bottom of the kitchen sink. The mat will give your cat something to hold and keep him from slipping. (The kitchen sink is small enough to allow you to hold onto the cat so that he can't escape. The bathtub is too big, and you won't be able to control him easily.)

- Fill the sink with a few inches (about 5-7 cm) of lukewarm water, and lightly wet your cat's fur.

- Rub a small amount of cat shampoo

into the fur and lather it well. Avoid getting any shampoo or water into your cat's eyes, ears, mouth, or nose.

- Fill a small cup with warm water and rinse the fur thoroughly. Make sure that you rinse well, because your cat will give himself a "cat bath" after his "human bath."

- Wrap your cat in a thick, fluffy towel and take him out of the sink. Dry him and keep him indoors and away from drafts until his coat dries. You may want to offer him a treat as a reward for good behavior.

If you've never bathed a cat before, ask a friend or relative to help you. One person can hold the cat securely while the other person concentrates on washing and rinsing. Kitten owners may be able to bathe their pets without a helper until the kitten grows to full size. If you are going to give your kitten a bath, adjust the depth of the water and the amount of shampoo accordingly.

Nail Care

Some owners trim (or clip) their cat's front claws once a month as part of the grooming ritual, but it's not absolutely necessary. (Many owners choose not to trim their cat's nails at all.) If your feline is using a scratching post on a regular basis, he is taking care of his own nails the natural way. However, if you want to trim his nails, you'll have to buy a nail clipper designed specifically for use on cats. (Never use nail clippers made for humans on cats or other pets.)

Most cats don't like having their feet touched and may resist having

their nails clipped. To get your feline accustomed to the procedure, periodically touch his paws and press lightly on the foot to extend the claws. Do this until he gets used to it and doesn't protest. When he becomes comfortable with you touching his feet, you can try trimming his nails.

To begin trimming the claws, hold your cat securely in your lap (or have a

FAMILY-FRIENDLY TIP

Kiddy Cat Groomers

If you have children in the home, they can help you groom the cat (depending on their ages). It's a good way for them to learn responsible pet care, and it will give them time to bond with him. A child of the appropriate age can help you brush or comb the cat (with supervision). Younger children can watch as you go through the grooming process. Encourage them to ask questions, and explain what you're doing and why.

Although a child can help brush the cat, never let her tend to the more complicated grooming tasks, such as bathing, nail trimming, teeth brushing, and ear cleaning. Your child could seriously injure the cat, and he will not readily accept being groomed again.

51

Trimming your cat's nails isn't absolutely necessary. If he is using a scratching post on a regular basis, he is taking care of his own nails the natural way.

he is young, he will learn to accept nail trimming as part of the grooming routine. However, don't force an adult cat who has never had his nails trimmed to undergo this ritual. It will stress him, and he may resent grooming time.

If you're unsure about how to trim your cat's nails or aren't sure if you should even try, talk to your veterinarian. She can discuss the subject with you and show you how to do it. If you take your cat to a professional pet groomer, she can perform the procedure for you.

Eye Care

A cat's eyes usually do not need much attention in the grooming department. If your cat has residue in the corners of his eyes, gently wipe it off with a cotton ball dipped in warm water. However, be careful not to touch the eye with the cotton ball. A cat's eyes are extremely sensitive, and you can scratch the eyelid or cause an ulcerated cornea. If something (such as dust, dirt, or hair) gets in the eye, flush it with saline solution and wipe around the corner (or edge) with a cotton ball or gauze. If your cat has a serious eye ailment, don't try to treat it at home—take him to the vet at once.

Ear Care

A healthy cat's ears only need a small amount of grooming maintenance. To determine if your cat needs to have his

friend hold him) and extend one of his feet. Gently press on one digit of the paw until the claw comes out. Trim off the white tip (about 1/8 or 1/4 of an inch [0.3 or 0.6 cm]). Do not cut into the quick, which is the pink part of the nail. This is where the nerves and blood vessels are. If you accidentally cut into the quick, apply a styptic pencil to the nail to stop the bleeding. Your cat will be upset because he is in pain, so you should end the grooming session at once. Give him some time to calm down before you try trimming another nail.

Start slowly, and only trim one or two claws at a time (or just one paw) until your cat gets used to the process. If you start the grooming procedure when ears cleaned, examine them gently. They should look clean inside, but if you see brown waxy residue, they need to be groomed.

Cats who shake their heads a lot and who always seem to be scratching their ears may have ear mites. If the ears smell bad, have chunks of dark wax, or look like they're filled with coffee grounds, your cat could have an ear infection or mites. In he displays any of these symptoms, take him to the vet. She will clean your cat's ears (and show you how to do it properly at home) and will give you prescription eardrops to kill the mites.

Keeping your cat's ears clean is a simple procedure that will prevent the ear mites from returning. About once a week (more often if your cat has long hair or ear curls), swab out the ears with a cotton ball dipped in baby oil or mineral oil. Use one cotton ball per ear, and repeat if necessary until the ear looks clean. If your cat hates having his ears groomed, you may want to have a friend hold him

Grooming the Older Cat

If you have a senior or geriatric cat, you may have to groom him every day. As cats age, they lose flexibility in their muscles and joints and may not be able to bend, stretch, and reach to wash themselves like they used to. This is why they often look unkempt or scraggly. Older cats also may lose interest in their appearance and won't wash as often as they once did.

You can help to keep your older cat looking great by gently brushing (or combing) him each day. Brushing helps to spread natural oils on the fur and prevents it from becoming dry and frazzled looking. It also increases blood circulation and stimulates the nervous system, which makes the cat feel good.

Seniors also may need to have their nails clipped. Some older cats do not use the scratching post as often as they used to, and their nails may become overgrown (especially on the hard-to-scratch-with back feet). If your cat has overgrown nails, he could get them snagged on furniture or carpets and harm himself while trying to pull free, or he could accidentally scratch himself too hard and draw blood.

If you need to give your older cat a bath, remember that seniors are more sensitive to heat and cold than younger cats. Keep the bathwater lukewarm (or what's most comfortable for your cat), and be sure to keep him warm until his fur dries completely.

Be gentle and don't rush when you're grooming your older cat. Take things slow and easy, and stop if he becomes upset, anxious, or scared. With the right amount of patience and love, you can keep your senior looking great for the rest of his life.

53

Looking Good

still or place him securely in your lap so that he cannot run away.

Never stick a cotton swab designed for cleaning out human ears in your cat's ear canal; you could cause serious damage to the eardrum. Using a long swab will push the dirt and wax farther down into the ears and makes cleaning harder. Always handle your cat's ears gently because they are very sensitive.

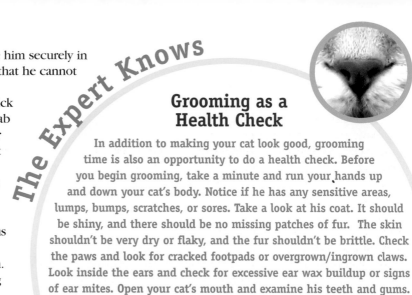

The Expert Knows

Grooming as a Health Check

In addition to making your cat look good, grooming time is also an opportunity to do a health check. Before you begin grooming, take a minute and run your hands up and down your cat's body. Notice if he has any sensitive areas, lumps, bumps, scratches, or sores. Take a look at his coat. It should be shiny, and there should be no missing patches of fur. The skin shouldn't be very dry or flaky, and the fur shouldn't be brittle. Check the paws and look for cracked footpads or overgrown/ingrown claws. Look inside the ears and check for excessive ear wax buildup or signs of ear mites. Open your cat's mouth and examine his teeth and gums. The gums should be pink and healthy, and there should be no missing or broken teeth. (If your cat has very bad breath, it could be a sign of gum disease or another ailment.) The eyes and nose should be clean and clear, not runny. Taking a few extra minutes to examine your cat before you groom him keeps him healthy and alerts you to any physical changes that may indicate a problem.

Dental Care

Practicing good dental hygiene on your cat prevents gum disease, tooth loss, and the buildup of tartar and plaque. If possible, begin a dental care routine when your cat is young or still a kitten so that he gets used to the process. An adult cat who has never had his teeth cleaned before will resist it, because cats don't like having their mouths or teeth touched—so be patient. If he refuses to let you brush his teeth, take him to the veterinarian and let her do it for you. She also can remove any hardened tartar and built-up plaque on the teeth.

Most vets recommend brushing a cat's teeth once a week.

Before you begin brushing, get your cat used to you working around his mouth by opening it and looking at his gums and teeth. To open his mouth, hold him in your lap (or have someone else hold him) and put your middle finger and thumb at the corners. Hook your fingers gently inside and tilt your cat's head back. When his mouth opens, look inside. (You also can peek inside when he yawns.) The gums should look pink and healthy, and the teeth should be intact. If you see pale, swollen, or bleeding gums or missing, cracked, or crooked teeth, take your cat to the vet right away.

After examining your cat's mouth, gather your dental care supplies. You should have a toothbrush or finger cap designed for cats, as well as feline-safe toothpaste. Most come in flavors such as tuna, chicken, or beef, so your cat should like the taste. Never use toothpaste designed for humans—it could make him seriously ill.

Now you're ready to brush your cat's teeth. Here's how: First, wet the toothbrush (or finger cap), then apply a tiny bit of toothpaste to it. Next, brush the teeth one row at a time. Don't scrub hard; just pass the toothbrush or finger cap lightly over the outside of the teeth. (You only need to clean the outside because a cat's rough tongue brushes the inside of the teeth.) There's no need to "rinse" his mouth because the toothpaste is edible.

Your cat may struggle a bit at first, but he should settle down when he realizes that the toothpaste tastes good. If he becomes too upset by the whole process, stop what you're doing and let him go. You can try again another time when he has calmed down.

Finding a Professional Pet Groomer

Some owners prefer to pay a professional pet groomer to tend to their cat's grooming needs. If you have a long-haired breed that needs severe mats or knots removed from his coat, you may have to hire a groomer to untangle his fur every so often. Many people who show their pedigreed cats at shows take their pets to the groomer before the big event so that they look their best.

One way to find a reputable groomer is to ask friends, relatives, and coworkers who own cats to recommend someone. If possible, find a "cats-only" groomer. She will have lots of experience dealing with cats, and your feline won't be frightened or distracted by the scents and sounds of dogs or other animals in the establishment.

Grooming as Bonding Time

Make grooming a pleasant time for your cat. Don't rush through the process and make him anxious, nervous, or afraid. When mother cats groom their kittens, they use the time to bond with them, and you can, too. This is a perfect opportunity for you to connect with your feline friend. Fussing over him will build trust and a strong love connection between the two of you. Cats love attention and affection, and most will welcome a gentle grooming. They like the feel of being brushed and will come to expect it daily.

Be patient with your cat when you groom him. Always treat grooming as a time to bond with him and fuss over him. Offer your cat a treat after every grooming session as a reward for being a good kitty.

Chapter 5

Feeling Good

Your cat or kitten is relying on you to give him a good home and to provide him with the best care possible for his entire life. It's up to you to make sure that he receives all the necessary veterinary checkups and vaccinations. The best way to keep your cat healthy is to find a veterinarian who will help you every step of the way, through each stage of his life.

Finding a Veterinarian

If you've never owned a cat before, don't worry—finding a vet is easy. Ask everyone you know who has a cat which vet they use and how they like the service. After you've gotten several recommendations, call each practice and explain that you're looking for a vet for your cat. Ask the following questions:

- Is it a "cats-only" clinic?

- Does the vet own cats?

- What are the clinic's regular hours? Does it offer night and weekend appointments?

- Is there a vet on-call in case of an after-hours emergency? (If not, what does the clinic recommend that you do with your pet?)

- What are the fees for office visits and vaccinations?

- What are the payment options?

Based on the answers you receive, you can either schedule an in-person meeting with the vet or keep searching. Remember that the professional whom you choose will be vital in maintaining the health of your cat. Take your time and find the *right* vet, not just *any* vet.

Once you've narrowed your choices down to two or three candidates, go to each office and talk to the staff,

A healthy diet, annual veterinary checkups, and up-to-date vaccinations should keep your cat in perfect health.

RECEPTION
PLEASE CHECK IN

ask for a tour of the facility, and meet the vet (if possible). Bring a list of questions that you have about her experience with cats, and discuss her practice, what veterinary association she belongs to, and if she also practices general animal care. Don't be shy about getting straight answers.

Choose a veterinarian who makes you feel comfortable, takes the time to talk with you, and answers your questions completely. After all, you're entrusting your cat to this professional *and* paying for the service. Evaluate the cleanliness of the office, including the exam rooms, and the helpfulness of the staff. If the staff acts impatient with you or other clients or doesn't want to answer your questions, move on and keep looking.

Some owners prefer to use a vet who specializes in feline medicine and has a "cats-only" practice. Such a vet has a lot of experience with feline medical issues and keeps up to date on the latest studies, procedures, and other cat-specific medical information. These vets also have "cat-sized" medical equipment and surgical supplies on hand, which makes the visit much less stressful for your cat. (Also, there won't be any barking dogs in the office.) If you find a feline-only veterinary clinic in your area, it's worth checking out to see if it meets with your approval.

After you've found the vet whom you're going to use, keep her name, address, phone number, office hours, and the directions to the clinic in a convenient place. If you or another family member has to take your

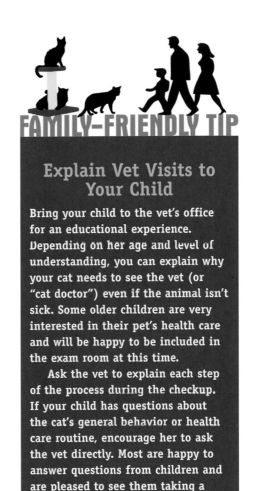

FAMILY-FRIENDLY TIP

Explain Vet Visits to Your Child

Bring your child to the vet's office for an educational experience. Depending on her age and level of understanding, you can explain why your cat needs to see the vet (or "cat doctor") even if the animal isn't sick. Some older children are very interested in their pet's health care and will be happy to be included in the exam room at this time.

Ask the vet to explain each step of the process during the checkup. If your child has questions about the cat's general behavior or health care routine, encourage her to ask the vet directly. Most are happy to answer questions from children and are pleased to see them taking a responsible role in pet care.

Feeling Good

cat in for medical attention, all the information will be easily accessible.

During treatment, if the vet recommends a surgical procedure or a remedy that you don't agree with, don't be shy about getting a second opinion. Ask another vet what the alternatives are, and ask for advice on the best course to take. Trust your instincts when it comes to your cat's health care. If you are dissatisfied with the vet's advice, if it seems questionable, or if a condition shows no sign of improvement, get a second opinion. Your cat will thank you for it.

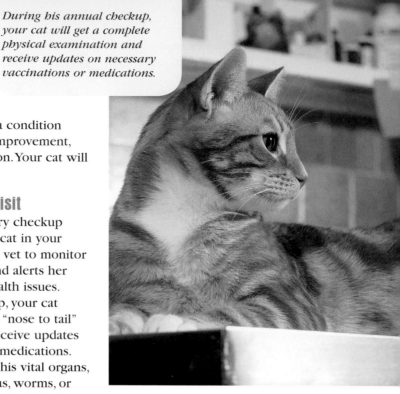

The Annual Vet Visit

An annual veterinary checkup is a must for every cat in your home. It allows the vet to monitor your cat's health and alerts her to any potential health issues. During the checkup, your cat will get a complete "nose to tail" examination and receive updates on vaccinations or medications. The vet will check his vital organs, inspect him for fleas, worms, or other parasites, examine him for lumps or growths, and check his teeth, weight, and temperature. Sometimes the vet will ask for a stool sample or draw blood for tests. This is a good time for you to ask any questions that you have about your cat's diet or to mention specific concerns that you have about his health.

Life Stages

Veterinary care will vary as your cat grows, matures, and ages. Kittens need to see the vet several times during their first year to get vaccinations and to be spayed or neutered. Because the body changes as cats age, older cats (including seniors and geriatrics) should get a complete physical twice a year.

Many cats start experiencing signs of aging at ten years old. As cats advance in age, their bodily functions slow down, and they undergo a general dulling of the senses. They sleep more, play less, and become more sensitive to temperature changes. Older cats also become more vulnerable to injury and disease because their immune systems are slowing down and becoming less efficient.

With aging, the heart doesn't pump as well. Circulation decreases, and the cat becomes more sensitive to the cold. The lungs lose their efficiency, making him prone to respiratory infections and other ailments. Kidney and liver function also decline, and there is an increased risk of disease, diabetes, urinary tract problems, and incontinence. Some older cats will have problems using the litter box.

Older cats also may develop brittle bones, joint or tendon pain or injury, loss of flexibility and mobility, and loss of muscle tone. They may not be able to jump up and down as they once did. Also, the coat thins out and becomes dull or gray. The claws become brittle and may need to be clipped to avoid becoming snagged on objects. Seniors may lose teeth or develop gum disease. Those with sensitive teeth may have a hard time chewing dry food. As a cat ages, his eardrums thicken, resulting in hearing loss, and he can develop cataracts and lose vision clarity.

Your feline companion can live an average of 15 to 19 years, so take good care of him. You're his best friend, and he's relying on you to make him comfortable in his golden years.

Vaccinations

It's important to vaccinate your cat against diseases. If you own a kitten, ask your vet which shots he needs and when. In general, kittens receive their first series of inoculations when they are approximately eight weeks old. The vet will schedule booster shots three to four weeks after the first series of vaccinations. As the kitten grows, he will need booster shots every year (or every three years, depending on the vaccination and the vet's recommendation).

Talk to your vet about the vaccination process, and ask her to explain each vaccination in detail.

Be sure you understand what each type is for and why your kitten needs (or doesn't need) it. Always ask

SENIOR CAT TIP

Vet Care for Senior Cats

When your cat reaches eight years of age, start him on a preventive health care program designed for older cats. This includes a complete physical checkup twice a year, including a dental exam. The vet will be able to detect any significant physical changes, look for signs of illness, and make sure that your cat is current on all necessary inoculations.

Ask if your older cat should be started on a special diet. Pet food manufacturers have developed senior formula blends of dry and canned food. Based on your cat's overall health, your vet may recommend adding vitamin or mineral supplements to his food. They will help to boost the immune system as well as help the body absorb nutrients.

If you have any questions about your cat's health care needs as he ages, speak with your vet. She may make recommendations regarding lifestyle changes that could benefit him in his senior years.

Feeling Good

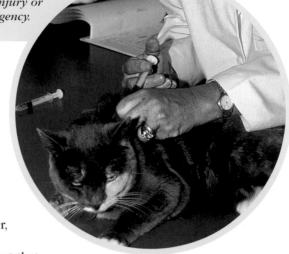

Every owner should be prepared to assist her pet in the case of an injury or medical emergency.

questions if you are confused about any aspect of your cat's health care needs.

It's always a good idea to get a medical history from your cat's former owner. This allows you to know all about his previous medical care. You'll know when he received his last physical and which vaccinations (if any) he's already had. However, if you adopt a stray and have no medical history for him, tell the vet that your cat needs a complete checkup and all necessary vaccinations. Don't assume that your adopted stray is healthy and disease-free.

Based on your cat's lifestyle (if he is an indoor-only cat or a single cat), the vet may recommend that you skip some vaccinations because he will not have had any exposure to disease. If you have a multiple-cat household, make sure that each one is vaccinated. One sick animal could make your healthy pets seriously ill.

Occasionally, kittens and adults have mild reactions to vaccinations. The symptoms include sneezing, fever, lethargy, and loss of appetite. Whenever your cat gets a vaccination, observe him after you bring him home from the vet's office and be alert for signs of a reaction. If he has a reaction or serious side effects such as vomiting or trouble breathing, take him back to the vet at once.

Neutering and Spaying

All cats should be spayed or neutered by the time they are six months of age. Cats who are neutered or spayed live longer, healthier lives than those who are left intact, and many generally become more affectionate.

Neutered (or castrated) males will not have a tendency to "spray" to mark their territory, and if they are allowed to go outside, they will not be as inclined to fight with other cats or wander the neighborhood. Neutering is a simple procedure and may require an overnight stay in the vet's office. Spaying a female is a little more involved and is often more expensive than neutering. She will undergo surgery to remove her reproductive organs and also will need to spend the night in the veterinary clinic. A spayed female will not go into "heat" or cry to

First Aid for Cats

If your cat becomes injured or stops breathing, would you know what to do? Every owner should be prepared to assist her pet in the case of an injury or medical emergency. While minor cuts and scrapes can be treated at home, use first aid to keep your cat alive until you can get him to the vet for medical treatment. Take your feline to the vet immediately if he is hit by a car, poisoned, shot, has any serious burns or bites, is attacked by an animal, or has any of the following:

- a deep cut or wound that won't stop bleeding
- a pus-filled wound and a fever
- a temperature over 105°F
- an eye injury
- bloody diarrhea or vomit
- broken bones or tail
- paralysis

Your vet can recommend a book devoted to first-aid care for cats that covers any possible scenario (such as how to set a broken bone or what to do if your cat is choking), but here are some first-aid basics for all pet owners:

- Keep a well-stocked first aid kit in an accessible location in your home. The kit should include adhesive tape, gauze pads, cotton balls/swabs, a rectal thermometer, petroleum jelly, mineral oil, topical antibiotic ointment, tweezers, hydrogen peroxide, and a small thick towel.

- Put the name, address, phone number, and directions to the vet's office or 24-hour emergency clinic near the telephone. Make sure that all family members know where it is.

- Learn how to perform CPR and mouth-to-mouth resuscitation on a cat (and kitten). Ask your vet to show you how to do this safely so that you don't accidentally harm your pet.

As a responsible pet owner, you need to be alert for any signs of illness and act quickly if you think your cat is sick.

be let out to look for a mate.

If you adopted your cat or kitten from an animal rescue organization or shelter, he may already be altered. Many pet organizations spay or neuter all animals they put up for adoption to avoid contributing to the pet overpopulation problem.

Signs of Illness

As intelligent as your cat is, he can't tell you if he's feeling sick. As a responsible pet owner, it's up to you to be alert for signs of illness and act quickly if you think he is sick. A drastic change in any area of his life (including eating or sleeping habits, change in general temperament, or "bad" litter box behavior) is a signal that something is wrong. If you know how your cat usually acts, you'll notice when he is not behaving normally.

If you think that your cat is ill, take him to the vet immediately. Don't wait and hope that he will get better on his own or that the problem will go away. Depending on the illness or medical problem, delaying treatment could be fatal, and in most cases, waiting makes the situation worse. It's better to be safe than sorry, so seek veterinary advice right away.

A list of common signs of illness follows. If your cat displays any of these symptoms, take him to the vet as soon as possible.

- bleeding
- bloated/distended stomach
- blood in urine or stool
- coughing
- crying, hissing, or growling when picked up or petted
- diarrhea
- discharge from the nose, ears, eyes, or anus
- drooling

- excessive eating or drinking
- fever
- labored or rapid breathing
- lethargy
- limping
- loss of appetite or will not drink
- rapid weight loss (or rapid weight gain)
- runny nose and/or discharge from the eyes
- straining in the litter box with no results
- sudden personality change (biting, scratching, or hissing)
- third eyelid (haw) exposed for a prolonged period of time
- trouble walking or walking off balance
- vomiting

General Illnesses

Health problems can range from something minor to a major life-threatening situation, and any sign of illness should be taken seriously. The following are some common health concerns.

Anemia

Anemia is caused by a low amount of red blood cells. These cells carry oxygen through the blood and are vital to a cat's health. A serious and sometimes fatal condition, anemia can indicate another illness. Cats with this disorder become oxygen starved and have a decreased appetite, increased respiration, and pale gums.

Bad Breath

Bad breath is a common sign of another ailment, which can include diabetes, cancer, tooth decay, or gum disease. If your cat has very bad breath, take him to the vet for a dental exam.

Cancer

Cancer is abnormal tissue growth, and if left unchecked, it will spread throughout the body. Although cancer can occur at any age, it is a common cause of death in older cats. Symptoms are growths or lumps on the skin that get bigger, trouble swallowing, lack of appetite, weight loss, excessive thirst, difficulty breathing, lethargy, bad breath, and wounds that don't heal.

Conjunctivitis

Conjunctivitis is an inflammation of the inner eyelid. The lining of the eye may appear pink or red and swollen. Yellow discharge is a common symptom. If your cat has any eye problems, take him to the vet right away.

Diabetes

Diabetes is caused by the failure of the pancreas to produce enough insulin to metabolize glucose. Older or obese cats with diabetes have high levels of glucose in their blood. Symptoms include excessive thirst, urination, and hunger. If left untreated, diabetes can cause blindness and kidney damage. Your vet will recommend treatment, which could include dietary changes, pills, or daily injections.

65

Diarrhea

A stomach virus, dairy products, overfeeding, stress, spoiled food, or a parasitic infection often cause diarrhea. Kittens and older cats are less hardy than adults, and diarrhea can cause life-threatening dehydration in them. If your cat has diarrhea, give him plenty of water and take him to the vet as soon as possible. She may inject your cat with fluids to prevent dehydration and take a blood or fecal sample to determine the cause of the problem.

Feline Immunodeficiency Virus (FIV)

This virus attacks the immune system and makes a cat susceptible to chronic infections. FIV is transmitted through saliva and bites. If your cat goes outdoors, you should consider having him vaccinated against FIV as a precaution. However, if he does get vaccinated, he will always test positive for the disease. This taints future testing for the rest of his life. If you have an indoor-only cat, you probably won't need to worry about him contracting this virus. Discuss FIV with your vet and see if your feline needs to be inoculated against it.

Feline Infectious Peritonitis (FIP)

There are two types of FIP. A cat who has the "dry" form will drink a lot of water because his kidneys are failing. A cat with the "wet" form will have trouble breathing because of fluid collection in the chest cavity or abdomen. This disease is common

Pet Insurance

Many owners purchase pet insurance for their cats. Pet health insurance companies write policies that work like human health insurance does. The owner pays a monthly or annual premium and submits claims as she incurs vet bills. After fulfilling the deductible requirements (which vary based on the policy and the amount of coverage), the owner is reimbursed for a percentage of her expenses. Before buying a policy, research the insurance company (to make sure they're legitimate and have a reliable reputation) and read the policy carefully so that you know what you're buying. It should explicitly state what veterinary services (such as spaying/neutering, dental care, lab costs, vaccinations, or emergency treatments) and procedures are covered and which ones aren't. If you're interested in buying a policy for your cat, ask your vet to recommend a reputable agency that specializes in this type of insurance.

in kittens and older cats because their immune systems aren't very strong. There is no cure for FIP. Some symptoms include an unkempt coat, loss of appetite, a swollen stomach, anemia, fever, and weight loss. If you have an indoor-only cat and he never comes into contact with other cats, your vet might recommend that you skip this inoculation.

Feline Leukemia Virus (FeLV)

FeLV is a highly contagious, deadly disease that attacks the immune system and makes it susceptible to disease. FeLV is passed from cat to cat through direct contact via saliva, urine, feces, and blood. A cat who drinks from the same bowl as an infected animal can become a carrier for the disease.

FeLV is extremely deadly to kittens, and about a third who contract it die. Kittens can contract FeLV if they nurse from an infected mother or come into contact with an infected kitten or cat. Vets give vaccinations against FeLV depending on the cat's risk of exposure (higher risk cats are those who were strays or who came from a shelter, cats who go outside, and cats who live in multiple-cat households) and his general health and age. Symptoms include excessive drinking, colds, lethargy, anemia, diarrhea, blood in the stool, loss of appetite, and weight loss.

If you already have a cat and get another one, always get the newcomer checked for FeLV before you bring him home. (Don't accidentally risk exposing a healthy cat or kitten to FeLV.) Some animal rescue organizations place FeLV-positive cats and kittens together in FeLV-positive cat households. These cats can live together comfortably for the rest of their lives.

Feline Panleukopenia Virus (FPV)

FPV is also known as feline distemper. This disease attacks the nervous system, immune system, and bowels. Ask your vet to immunize your cat or kitten against FPV.

A healthy cat can contract FPV from a sick cat or from infected fleas. If you handle a cat with FPV and then pet your healthy cat, you could accidentally transmit FPV to him. (As a precaution, always wash your hands after handling an unfamiliar or sick cat or after emptying the litter box. You don't want to unwittingly transmit a disease to your healthy pet.) Symptoms of FPV include lethargy, loss of appetite, and lack of balance. If your cat is displaying these symptoms, take him to the vet immediately.

Feline Respiratory Disease Complex (FRDC)

FRDC includes upper respiratory infections such as colds, flu, and feline pneumonia. Symptoms include discharge from the eyes and nose and sneezing. Feline pneumonia is a contagious bacterial infection that can be passed from cat to cat. Symptoms include congestion, difficulty breathing, sneezing, coughing, fever, shortness of breath, and yellow/green nasal discharge. It is common in kittens and older cats and should be treated by a veterinarian.

Feline Urologic Syndrome (FUS) or Feline Lower Urinary Tract Disease (FLUTD)

FUD or FLUTD is a serious problem. A cat with FUS (or FLUTD) could be suffering from bladder or urethral stones or blockages. Symptoms include crying when trying to urinate, urine retention, inability to urinate or straining while trying to urinate, blood or pus in the urine, a hard, full bladder, and constant licking of the genital area.

Because the cat cannot urinate, high levels of deadly toxins build up in his blood. An acute blockage can lead to uremic poisoning and can be fatal if not treated within 48 hours.

Urinary tract infections (UTI) have similar symptoms (difficulty urinating, bloody urine, or urinating outside the litter box) and often affect males. Cystitis is an inflammation of the lining of the bladder. The obstruction prevents the cat from urinating and causes FUS. It is common in older cats, and approximately 1 to 2 percent of the feline population suffers from it. If your cat has any of these symptoms or trouble urinating, take him to the vet immediately.

Fleas

Fleas are external parasites that bite into a cat's skin and suck his blood. A serious flea infestation can make an adult cat anemic and could be deadly to a kitten. In addition to draining blood, fleas also can infect your cat with tapeworms. Although fleas are common on pets, their presence shouldn't be dismissed lightly. In six months, fleas can lay thousands of eggs on your pet and in your home.

To see if your cat has fleas, part his fur and look for something that resembles black flecks of pepper. (You might even see the fleas crawling on him.) If your cat has fleas, take him to the vet and she will recommend the best treatment. Today there are many remedies available, including flea shampoos, dips, and "spot-on" treatments. Don't treat the fleas yourself without consulting a vet. Some flea preventives may be too strong for kittens less than 12 weeks of age. Never use a flea product designed for dogs on a cat—it could be fatal.

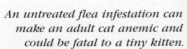

An untreated flea infestation can make an adult cat anemic and could be fatal to a tiny kitten.

Declawing

Some owners who cannot stand the thought of their cats scratching the furniture have them declawed, a permanent procedure that surgically removes the claws. Although it's natural for cats to scratch, some owners use declawing as a way to correct what they believe are bad scratching behaviors. What these owners don't realize is that in addition to making the cat defenseless, it affects the way he walks and throws him off balance.

Declawing a healthy cat can be dangerous. Most owners do not realize that the cat is undergoing surgery. As with any surgery, there's always the risk that the animal could have a negative reaction to the anesthetic. If the surgery isn't done properly, the cat could develop an ingrown claw (or claws), which would require additional surgery. Most cats do not like to wear post-surgical bandages on their feet and tear them off (or rip out their stitches), which can lead to excessive bleeding, infection, or the need to have the feet restitched and rebandaged.

Many cats who have been declawed suffer psychological problems. They may develop distrust for their owners, become confused as to why their feet hurt, and not understand why they can no longer scratch anything. Some become aggressive toward other pets or humans in the home and resort to biting as a means of defense. Others become depressed and are never quite the same.

Many veterinarians refuse to perform declawing surgery and recommend having the nails trimmed instead. Be kind to your cat or kitten, and don't force him to undergo this cruel procedure.

Kidney Disease

The kidneys filter the blood and help excrete waste. If they are not functioning properly, deadly toxins build up in the blood and can lead to a coma or death. (In essence, the cat is poisoned by a buildup of waste and toxins in the blood, a condition called chronic renal failure.)

Kidney problems are common in older cats, so ask your vet to check your senior's kidney function during the annual exam. Causes of kidney disease include tumors, kidney injury, kidney stones, or diabetes. Symptoms include loss of appetite, weight loss, lethargy, high blood pressure, vomiting, and increased thirst or urination.

Liver Disease

The liver regulates the chemicals in the body, controls metabolism, processes fats and carbohydrates, and rids the body of toxins. It also manufactures proteins, bile, and blood-clotting factors. Liver function slows as cats age, and liver disease is common in older cats. Liver failure is life-threatening. With aging, the risk of developing liver problems increases. Causes of liver disease include parasitic infections, dietary deficiencies, tumors, and hepatitis. Signs of liver disease or failure include lack of appetite, a distended abdomen, increased thirst, dark urine, vomiting, weight loss, and diarrhea.

Rabies

Rabies is a deadly virus that attacks the nervous system, spinal cord, and brain. It is transmitted through saliva when the victim is bitten but can also enter the bloodstream through a scratch. Symptoms can appear one week to one year after the initial bite and include aggression, headaches, and trouble swallowing. A rabid animal may attack anything or anyone who comes too close. Make sure that your cats are vaccinated against rabies, especially if they go outside and could have contact with other animals.

Tapeworms

Tapeworms are long, flat worms that release their eggs into the feces of infected animals. These parasites live in the intestines of kittens and cats and rob the body of nutrients. If left untreated, a tapeworm infestation can be fatal to a small kitten. Tapeworms cause anemia, diarrhea, abdominal pain, an increased appetite, weight loss, and lethargy.

A cat who has fleas also may have tapeworms, and he could swallow tapeworm eggs when he grooms himself. If you suspect that your cat has a tapeworm, lift the tail and check the area around the anus. If you spot white or yellow rice-like worms moving under the base of his tail or anus, take him to the vet and ask for a deworming treatment.

Ticks

Ticks are small brown/black external parasites. These bloodsuckers drain the cat of blood and spread disease. If your pet isn't allowed outside, he shouldn't come into contact with ticks. If he does go outside, part his fur in various places and check him. (Ticks often hide in the ears and on the neck.)

If you find a tick on your cat, grasp the body with tweezers and pull it out slowly. Don't use matches, alcohol, salt, or other home remedies to try to remove the tick because you could seriously harm your pet. If your cat has a lot of ticks, or if you feel

Many cat owners prefer holistic veterinary medicine because it does not use drugs, chemicals, chemotherapy, or other treatments that harm the system.

uncomfortable pulling them off, take him to the vet and have them professionally removed.

Toxoplasmosis

This protozoan infects the intestines. Signs of toxoplasmosis include blood or mucus in the stool, diarrhea, and vomiting. If you suspect that your cat has toxoplasmosis, take him to the vet at once. Small kittens can die from a severe case of this infection.

Upper Respiratory Infections

While upper respiratory infections (or colds) are not a major concern for adult cats, they can be troublesome to a small kitten. Kittens should be vaccinated against the most common cold viruses (feline calicivirus and feline herpesvirus) as soon as possible. An infected kitten can spread the illness to other animals in the household, so if yours has a cold, keep him isolated from other pets for 7 to 14 days. Symptoms of a feline cold are lack of appetite, lack of energy, sneezing, a runny nose, and watery eyes.

Alternative Therapies

If you're interested in alternative therapies or holistic treatments for your cat, consult a holistic vet. Holistic medicine focuses on helping the body and mind restore itself to a normal, balanced state so that it can fight off illness. Cat owners are slowly embracing the concept of holistic veterinary medicine by combining it with more conventional veterinary treatments. (According to a recent survey, 9 percent of cat owners use homeopathic or holistic remedies on their pets.) If you'd like to learn more about alternative or holistic treatments, the best place to start is with a holistic vet.

Holistic Veterinarians

Holistic veterinarians practice holistic or complementary veterinary medicine. In contrast, "conventional" veterinary medicine focuses on managing the body by treating physical injury or trauma, providing vaccinations, or prescribing antibiotics. A holistic vet treats the whole cat (mind, body, and emotions) and the cause of the illness or disease, not just the symptoms. Unlike conventional medicine, holistic medicine does not use drugs, chemicals, chemotherapy, or other treatments that harm the system. For example, a holistic vet may recommend vitamin or mineral supplements to boost the immune system during an illness, or she may speed the healing process along with herbal or plant remedies.

When presented with an ill cat, the holistic vet will explore every aspect of his life, including diet, home environment, exercise, and other pets in the home, and recommend changes that will achieve balance in all areas. Holistic medicine places an emphasis on natural foods, including vitamins, minerals, and a diet free from preservatives or chemicals.

If you'd like to find a holistic vet in your area and you can't get recommendations from friends or family, contact the American Holistic Veterinary Medical Association (AHVMA) at www.ahvma.org. Your chosen vet should be willing and able to answer any of your questions about holistic medicine or treatments. If your cat has a specific health concern or issue, ask the vet what natural treatments are available and what she recommends. Ask about potential side effects, and decide for yourself if the treatment is right for you and your cat.

Types of Alternative Therapies

Alternative therapies (such as acupuncture, acupressure, aromatherapy, botanical medicine, herbs, homeopathic medicine, massage therapy, and chiropractic therapy) are designed to help return the body to a natural state of balance. Many are used to treat chronic pain, behavioral disorders,

and degenerative diseases. There are numerous books and websites devoted to alternative therapies for felines. A holistic vet can discuss the different treatments with you in detail.

Acupuncture

Acupuncture is a form of Chinese healing that is based on the principle that energy (chi) flows through channels (or meridians) in the body. If the chi is blocked, pain, disease, or illness may result. Acupuncture works by inserting needles into the body along the meridian that leads to the blocked area. The treatment causes the body to release endorphins (natural painkillers), which temporarily relieves the pain and discomfort.

Before trying feline acupuncture, make sure that the person (preferably a vet) is qualified and experienced in working with cats, and get several references. Acupuncture is often used in conjunction with massage therapy and chiropractic therapy to treat pain caused by injury (such as a car accident or fall) or arthritis.

Bach Flower Remedies

Bach flower remedies are flower essences that are used to treat

Your cat depends on you to provide him with the best care possible for his entire life.

emotional or behavioral problems. The 38 flower essences have different therapeutic properties, and each addresses a specific behavior problem or emotional state.

Chiropractic Therapy

Chiropractic medicine originated in 1895 in Canada, and in 1996 the American Veterinary Association (AVA) declared that it was beneficial for pets. As with chiropractic medicine designed for people, the affected areas of the spine are manipulated and palpated by a qualified, trained professional. Chiropractic therapy can help cats with misaligned vertebrae, pinched nerves, or herniated discs. It is often used in conjunction with massage therapy to soothe injured muscles or joints. Treatments may help cats who were hurt in a car accident or a fall.

Homeopathic Medicine

Developed in Vienna in the late 1800s, homeopathic medicine is a complex system of medicine that boosts the immune response. Small doses of animal, mineral, or vegetable substances are derived through a process called "potentization," which releases therapeutic or healing properties. These are then used to stimulate the body's natural defenses to heal itself.

Massage Therapy

Massage therapy reduces stiffness in joints, muscles, and tendons. The light touch helps to restore mobility and flexibility to muscles and joints. Massage stimulates lymph and blood circulation, lowers blood pressure, lessens anxiety and stress, and boosts the immune system. (It's also a great way to bond with your cat!) Some cats love to be massaged, while others don't. Several books are available that show you how to do cat massage at home, or your vet can show you the basics. If you do your own massage, keep the sessions to five to ten minutes and stop if your cat becomes agitated.

Some Basic Rules About Alternative Therapies

Don't force your cat to have any alternative therapy or treatment that he doesn't want. Doing so will only make him distrust you, stress him, and may worsen the ailment or problem.

Always get references and recommendations before employing the services of any alternative therapist or holistic vet. Be sure that the person is certified and experienced in working with cats.

Also, ask a lot of questions before agreeing to any type of alternative therapy. Find out how many sessions are required, the costs involved, how you can tell if the therapy is working, and what your cat will be experiencing at each session.

You are your cat's best friend, and you owe it to him to take good care of him for the rest of his life. Giving him the proper care that he needs to stay healthy is easy. Regular veterinary checkups, vaccinations, and lots of love will keep your feline companion in good health for many years to come.

Chapter 6

Being Good

Your cat should be well adjusted and behave around family members and other pets. Believe it or not, cats can communicate with their owners through body language and vocalizations, and they can even learn tricks. All cats develop differently and have varying socialization needs. Some may be very outgoing and feel the urge to socialize more than others.

our cat must learn the rules of socialization so that he can interact with family members and other people. Socialization also helps you bond with your feline companion and develop a close, loving relationship.

Socializing Cats With Children

Most problems occur because children don't know how to behave around cats. They must be taught that a cat is a living animal who should be treated kindly. Teach them not to pet the cat too hard or against the lie of his fur, pull his tail or ears, hit or tease him, or chase him around the house for fun.

Cats and children can get along fine in the same household as long as certain rules are followed. First and foremost, no child under the age of three should be left alone with a cat or kitten. At this age, the child will not understand that the cat is a real animal with feelings and may see him as a stuffed toy. If the child does something to hurt the cat or refuses to put him down, the cat will use his claws to get away. Instruct children to leave the family pet alone when he is eating, sleeping, or using the litter box.

Preschoolers and toddlers should always be supervised when playing with, petting, or picking up any pet. You can teach them about cats from a very early age. Read age-appropriate books about cats to them, or visit people who have them. Children who live with cats should always be shown how to interact with them

The age at which children should be allowed to interact and bond with a pet depends on their maturity level and the personality of the pet.

How to Pick Up a Cat

It's crucial for owners to know how to pick up and handle a cat safely. Here's how:

- Approach your cat slowly and talk to him so that he knows that you're there.
- With the cat facing away from you, slip one hand under his chest (near the shoulders) and the other hand under the hindquarters. This gives him a feeling of stability and comfort. Make sure that his legs don't dangle free in midair.
- Bring your cat close to your chest or shoulder. Use one hand or arm to support his hindquarters and the other hand to pet him.

Cats enjoy being held by people they trust. If they don't feel comfortable being held, they'll squirm and want to be put down. If your cat struggles, set him down gently on the floor. Don't try to restrain or hold a cat who wants to be set free.

appropriately. They need to realize that these are delicate animals who are much smaller than they are, so they should be handled with care. Children must be taught to be especially careful around kittens, because these tiny creatures could inadvertently get stepped on and injured. A child could accidentally injure an adult cat by picking him up wrong, dropping him, or squeezing him. If your child plays too rough with the pet, separate them and give the cat some quiet time alone. Teach your children to ask permission before touching anyone's pets.

The age at which children should be allowed to interact and bond with a pet depends on their maturity level and the personality of the pet. Use your best judgment and evaluate the situation based on what you know about your child and the cat. Once children mature and understand how to properly handle the family pet, they can be left alone with him.

If you do not have children, your cat may avoid any youngsters who visit your home. If he decides to leave the room when children visit, don't try to force him to stay and "be friendly." Some cats never warm up to children because they see them as loud and noisy. Others will welcome the attention and will want to play with their newfound friends.

Socializing Cats With Other Cats

If you already have a cat and bring home a new cat or kitten, introduce them to each other slowly. Cats are territorial, and the established cat may hiss or growl at a strange cat in "his" house. Kittens aren't usually territorial toward another kitten, and they may immediately run off to play together. However, if you introduce a kitten to an adult cat, the kitten may be afraid of the bigger cat until they get to know each other.

If you have other pets, introduce them to your new cat slowly so they have time to get to know each other.

To introduce cats, place the new cat in his carrier and let the two cats see and sniff each other through the carrier door. Then place the established cat in his carrier and allow the new cat to wander around the house and sniff the other cat. You can also let the established cat sniff the new arrival under a door. This will allow them to get to know each other's scent and prevent any fighting.

When you feel that the two cats are ready to meet, introduce them to each other in a neutral place. Watch how they interact, and be prepared for some growling, hissing, or swiping. (This is natural.) When the cats become familiar with each other, they will establish a hierarchy and accept one another. As a precaution, don't leave the cats alone until you're sure they

won't fight. If they seem very agitated with each other, separate them and reintroduce them again the next day.

Once the cats have learned to get along, spend time petting, grooming, or playing with each cat in turn so that one does not get jealous of the other. When a new cat is introduced into the home, the established cat may feel like he is being replaced, which could lead to behavioral problems such as aggression or depression. Reassure the established cat that he's loved. Pet him a lot, play with him often, and give him extra attention. Don't show favoritism to the new cat or kitten or ignore your other cat.

Socializing Cats With Other Pets

Cats are very territorial and may highly resent other animals moving into their

Communicating With Your Cat

Understanding your cat is the best way to develop a strong relationship, build trust, and form a lifelong bond. Some owners instinctively know what their cat is thinking or feeling based on the flick of an ear or a twitch of the tail. These clever owners have learned the cat's body language. (For example, a cat who is feeling neglected, rejected, or jealous will sit with his back to his owner.) Cats also use body language to communicate with each other and have a universal set of body movements that all felines understand.

Learning cat body language is a great way to get inside your cat's mind and understand his thoughts and moods. You can interpret what your feline is thinking and feeling based on his vocalizations and the position of his ears, eyes, whiskers, and tail. Here are examples of cat "communication" and what they mean:

Eyes: Wide open—cat is alert, curious.
Half-closed—cat is napping or relaxed.
Pupils dilated—cat is frightened or alert.
Pupils are narrow slits—cat is annoyed.
Staring at you intently—cat distrusts you or is annoyed.
A long slow "blink" directed at you—this is known as a cat "kiss" and is a form of affection.

Ears: Upright and perked, facing front—cat is curious, happy, playful, and alert.
Facing backward—cat is worried or annoyed.
To the side—cat is fearful, distrusting, or annoyed.
Flat against the head—cat is aggressive and angry, or afraid.

Whiskers: Bent forward—cat is alert.
Fan out at sides—cat is relaxed.
Backward, flat against face—cat is scared, angry, or defensive.

Tail: Puffed out—cat is afraid or excited.
Slow wagging, waving, or relaxed—cat is content.
Thumping or swishing—cat is annoyed or angry. (The faster the thumping or swishing, the more that the cat is getting annoyed or angry.)
Raised straight up—a sign of greeting; cat is happy and is saying hello to you.
Lowered, tucked between legs—cat is scared or showing a sign of submission.

Vocalizations: Growl or hiss—cat is angry.
Meow—cat wants attention.
Mew—a soft meow, used when asking for something or saying hello.
Yowl—a very loud, insistent, demanding meow means that the cat is hungry and/or wants your attention "now!"
Chirp—a cat's way of greeting his owner (sounds like "chrrrp" or "brrrp").

Scientists believe that cats have over 100 different vocalizations, but experts cannot agree on how a cat purrs. Some scientists speculate that cats purr through a set of false vocal chords, while others think that muscle contractions in the chest are responsible for the sound. Experts also do not know exactly why cats purr or what it means. Cats purr when they are happy, relaxed, and content, yet they also purr when they are hurt or stressed.

Some breeds of cat (such as the Siamese) are very vocal and love to talk. Cats can produce what's called a "silent meow." This occurs when a feline opens his mouth and meows but no sound comes out. Scientists believe that the cat actually does produce sound, but it's at a level that's too high for humans to hear. Nobody knows what the "silent meow" means or why cats produce it.

Meeting a New Cat

When you or your children come into contact with someone's new pet cat, make introductions slowly (after getting permission from the owner, of course!). Here's how:

- Bend down to the cat's level and address him by name in a soothing voice.
- Make brief eye contact and extend your hand for the cat to sniff. If he comes to you, let him sniff you. (This is his way of meeting a new person, and he's also checking you out.)
- If the cat rubs against you, you're accepted and you can pet him. The best areas to pet are the back, sides, head, and the base of the tail. Some cats do not like their ears, stomachs, tails, or feet touched, so you should avoid these areas.

If the cat likes you and wants to visit, he will come closer and accept your attention. If he leaves, he's not interested in you and does not want to be petted. Never grab a cat to pet him, and don't try to force a cat to stay if he doesn't want to—he won't appreciate it.

home. If you have dogs, birds, or small animals, you'll have to make special arrangements for them to coexist with your new pet.

If you have a dog, your new cat or kitten will probably be terrified by him (especially if the cat has never lived in a home with dogs or has seen dogs before). Introduce him to the dog gradually. Let the dog sniff the cat under a door so that they become accustomed to each other's scent. After a day or two, place the cat in his carrier so that he can see and smell the dog from a safe place.

When you feel the time is right, bring your cat out and let the two animals meet. Don't leave them alone together until you're sure that there is not going to be a fight. Some dogs and cats learn to live together, while others have problems establishing territorial boundaries and

prefer to live in separate areas of the house. You can best determine if your dog will accept a cat—and if your new cat will like living with a dog.

If you have small animals, reptiles, birds, or fish, you might not want to introduce them to your cat. Because cats are natural hunters, they may see your guinea pig or bird as prey or a toy. (The other pet may feel threatened and develop stress if he comes into contact with the cat.) If you allow your cat access to the room(s) in which you house other pets, make sure that the cages or tanks are secure and that the cat cannot get into them.

Litter Box Training

One reason people love living with cats is because they have a natural instinct to use the litter box. When it comes to litter box training, the process is pretty simple.

When you bring your new cat home, show him where the litter box is. Pick him up and place him in it. He may sniff around and scratch a little, or he may use the box right away. Once he knows where the litter box is, don't move it. If you do, you will confuse him and he could have an "accident." If you must move it, show your cat where you've put it. Don't expect him to find it on his own.

When setting up the litter box, choose a quiet location that doesn't get a lot of household traffic or noise. A good place to keep it is in a spare bedroom or bathroom. Make sure that the door to the room is always open so your cat can use it at all times. Don't place it near his food or water dishes. Cats do not like to soil near where they eat. Instruct family members (especially children) to leave your cat alone when he's using the litter box.

Clean the litter box every day (even if you use clumping litter). One of the most common reasons that cats develop litter box problems is because the box isn't clean. Some will stop using it if you change brands or types of litter. To avoid this, try to buy the same litter your cat was using before he moved in with you. If you must change brands or types, gradually mix a blend of the old and new litter until he becomes accustomed to the new brand.

Being Good

Because cats have a natural instinct to use the litter box, the training process is fairly simple.

Treats for Training

The treats used as a reward should be something special that your cat loves but doesn't get when he's not training. Treats can be small morsels (pea-sized portions) of canned cat food, a cat treat, or a bit of tuna or cheese. To keep things interesting, change the flavor or type of treat every few days so that your cat gets an unexpected surprise. Make sure that you are providing something healthy, and never overfeed treats!

If you have more than one cat, each should have his own litter box. (Cats are territorial and do not like to share.) Keep the boxes in separate rooms or far enough apart so that each cat has a sense of privacy.

Tricks

Contrary to popular thought, you *can* teach your cat tricks. Some are even eager to learn and will look forward to training time. Others may not be interested in learning and will not respond to trick training. Don't try to turn your cat into something he isn't. You won't be able to force him to learn anything or do anything if he doesn't want to.

Some owners teach their cats "fancy" tricks such as rolling over, fetching, jumping through hoops, sitting up, or shaking hands. Other cat owners teach their cats "practical" tricks that are useful in everyday life such as coming when called or walking on a leash.

Training requires time, patience, and consistent reinforcement on your part. Cats will learn if you teach them, and some go on to have "showbiz" careers. There are entire books and websites devoted to trick training, but the basics are discussed here.

What's My Motivation?

Unlike dogs, cats do not have an innate need to please their owners or obey commands. They have their own reasons for doing things. In most cases, they need to be asked (or persuaded) to do something. The easiest way to motivate your self-interested cat is to make the action worth his while. This is best accomplished with a bribe of some kind—usually food. If you feed your cat on a regular feeding schedule, it will be easier to train him with a food reward. Schedule your training sessions about an hour before feeding time, when your cat is hungry, and he will be an alert student.

How to Train a Cat

First, buy a clicker, which is available from a pet supply store. A clicker is a piece of plastic with a metal tab that makes a loud "click" sound when pressed. The clicker will help your cat associate the "click" sound with the completion of the right move and the reward (a treat) that follows. You also will need to have a small supply of healthy treats on hand to use as rewards.

Training your cat to come to his name is a simple trick, and it's a good way to expand your pet's intellect while reinforcing the bond between you. It will also come in handy if you need to find your cat or want him to come to you. Many owners are surprised to discover that their cat has taught himself to come when called— without any formal training sessions. This is one of the easiest tricks to teach a cat, and it's a good foundation for learning other tricks.

To teach a cat to come to his name, go into another room and call him. (Keep calling until he comes.) When he comes, click the clicker. Then praise him and give him the reward. Repeat the training several times in one room, and then move to different rooms in the house. In time, your cat will learn to come when called because he has associated his name with something pleasant— a reward.

You also can train your cat to come when called and then have him go into his carrier. To do this, train him to come to his name and give him his reward inside the carrier. Your cat will associate the carrier with the treat.

Being Good

Cats who do not get enough play or interaction with their owners can become bored, restless, and develop behavior problems.

Cats

FAMILY-FRIENDLY TIP

Playing With Cats

Involving children in playtime with the family pet will help to create a strong bond between them and teaches them to see the cat as a friend. Show your child games that she can play with the cat, such as swatting a ping-pong ball back and forth or chasing a piece of string. Allow her to learn by example by letting her see you play with the cat. Always supervise young children when they are playing with pets to make sure that they don't accidentally play too roughly or hurt them.

Training Tips

Here are a few tips to make training successful:

- Keep training sessions fun. Never scold or hit your cat.

- Use your cat's name often when praising him. ("Good job, Inky!")

- Practice twice a day for five to ten minutes at the same time every day.

- Practice in a quiet place that's free from distractions.

- Let your cat learn one trick completely before building on it or teaching something new.

- Click the clicker immediately after

your cat does what you want him to do.

- Practice training when your cat is alert and hungry.

- Always end training sessions on a positive note and with a treat.

Daily Playtime

All cats and kittens need daily playtime. Cats who do not get enough play or interaction with their owners can become bored, restless, and develop behavior problems. (A bored cat will find ways of amusing himself, such as eating your plants.)

Set aside 10 to 15 minutes every day to play with your feline friend. Your cat will look forward to your scheduled playtime and will miss it if you skip a day. Play not only makes your pet socialized, but it's a great way to give him the exercise he needs while keeping his mind and instincts sharp.

Kittens need little or no encouragement to play and often play so hard that they wear themselves out. If you have more than one kitten in the house, you won't have to worry about scheduling playtime—kittens will play with each other constantly throughout the day.

Make sure that your cat has plenty of safe toys to play with. Leave the toys out when you're not home so that he can amuse himself during the day. Every so often, buy a new toy and introduce it to your cat, and then rotate out an old toy. He will find the new toy interesting, and in a few days you can bring back the old toy. Your cat will think the "old" toy is new again.

Cats love to play games, and you can throw a ping-pong ball down the hallway and have your cat chase it or swat a plastic ball for your cat to hit back to you. They also love cardboard boxes and may use them as toys, a scratching post, and as a bed. Your cat may also invent his own games of "chase" or tag with you or other pets.

A happy, well-socialized cat is a dream to have in the home. Cat lovers know that their cat is not a statue meant to be ignored and realize that the more they socialize with their pet, the more interest he will take in his owners' activities. Cats are intelligent animals who need stimulation and interaction in their world. Spend some quality time socializing with your feline companion, and see what he is trying to tell you—you may be surprised by what you learn!

Quality Time

Having a well-adjusted and happy cat can make all the difference when sharing your life and home with him. Spending daily quality time with him is important, and understanding his thoughts, moods, and behaviors is a great way to establish a loving bond between you. Animal behaviorists believe that the more time you spend interacting with your feline friend, the closer your relationship will be and the more communication you'll establish. This will increase trust between you, and your cat will become more affectionate toward you.

85

Chapter 7

Up a Tree

Cats are intelligent animals who can learn to understand the rules of living with people. However, sometimes your well-behaved feline may appear to "act up" for no apparent reason. Getting to the root of the problem and understanding why he is acting out is the best way to correct the unwanted behavior and return harmony to the household.

Why Cats Misbehave

Cats do not misbehave out of spite. They simply do things that seem natural or make sense to them. To correct problem behaviors, the owner must figure out what her cat is trying to communicate and then redirect the unwanted behavior toward an acceptable positive behavior. With patience and consistent reinforcement, the cat will make the connection and the "bad" behavior will be changed.

No matter what your cat does wrong, *never* yell at him or hit him—this will not make him correct his mistake. Striking any animal is cruel and will make him distrust you (which could lead to more behavioral problems).

To modify your cat's behavior, you must catch him in the act of doing the "wrong" thing, correct him, and then show him what he should be doing instead. Try to correct the unwanted behavior as soon as you notice it, because the longer the habit continues, the harder it will be to break. In time and with enough reinforcement, your cat will learn what you expect of him.

Boredom is a common cause of bad behavior. Usually, as soon as a bored pet has his attention redirected, the unwanted behavior stops. Acting out is a lonely cat's way of asking you to pay attention to him. Schedule regular playtimes with him and give him a lot of attention to alleviate his lack of stimulation. Having fun toys around so that he can amuse himself is another way of keeping him out of trouble.

Any sudden behavior changes in your cat's normal personality should be watched closely. If two or more "bad" behaviors crop up suddenly, it could be a sign of a medical condition, and he should then be taken to the vet for a physical exam.

The Expert Knows

Finding an Animal Behaviorist

If you feel that you need to employ the services of an animal behaviorist, discuss the issue with your veterinarian. She can most likely recommend a trained professional who specializes in cats. Behaviorists are experts in animal behavior and motivation and will be able to give you advice on how to solve your pet's problem. Make an appointment to talk with the behaviorist and explain your cat's behavior issues, the symptoms, and any methods that you've used to try to solve the problem on your own. Ask about her experience in treating your cat's problem. Be sure to get references, find out how many treatment sessions your cat may need, and ask what follow-up training (if any) you will have to do on your own at home. Many behaviorists make house calls and may want to observe the cat in his natural surroundings to better understand the unwanted behavior.

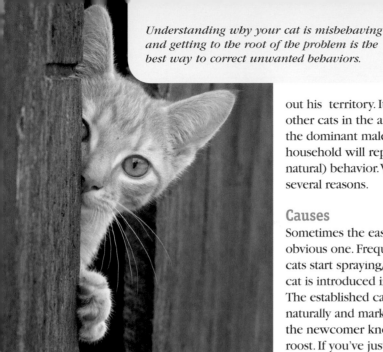

Understanding why your cat is misbehaving and getting to the root of the problem is the best way to correct unwanted behaviors.

Housesoiling/Spraying

It's not pleasant when a cat suddenly starts leaving messes on the floor or spraying urine on the walls. Owners who are frustrated with housesoiling and spraying often punish the cat by rubbing his nose in the mess—which only makes the problem worse. In some cases, the frustrated owner drops the cat off at an animal shelter because she feels that he is "out of control." Housesoiling/spraying is the number-one reason why many cats are abandoned at animal shelters.

To figure out why your pet is suddenly misbehaving, you need to understand him. In the wild, male cats mark their territories by spraying trees and other objects with urine so that other cats in the area know who's boss. Although cats usually bury their feces, a feline who needs to feel dominant will leave his waste uncovered as a way of staking out his territory. It's his way of letting other cats in the area know that he's the dominant male. Sometimes cats in a household will repeat this unwanted (yet natural) behavior. Why? There could be several reasons.

Causes

Sometimes the easiest answer is the most obvious one. Frequently, well-behaved cats start spraying/soiling when another cat is introduced into the household. The established cat does what comes naturally and marks his territory to let the newcomer know who rules the roost. If you've just moved to a new house, your cat may soil or spray because he smells the scent of a previous cat (or dog) on the carpet or on the walls. Again, he is trying to prove dominance over the other cat's scent.

Unneutered males feel the urge to start marking their territory as they reach sexual maturity. Having your cat neutered should solve this problem. A cat also may start spraying or housesoiling because of a medical condition, such as a bladder infection or blockage, or a kidney problem. If a new cat hasn't been introduced into the household, and your kitty starts spraying or leaving messes, call the veterinarian and schedule a complete physical. It's best to rule out any potential medical condition early.

Litter box problems are a common cause of housesoiling and spraying. If the litter box is dirty, if the cat does not like the litter, or if another cat (or a

89

Up a Tree

Boredom is a common cause of misbehavior, so having plenty of toys around to amuse your cat will keep him out of trouble.

person) is bothering him while trying to use the box, he will avoid it and eliminate elsewhere.

Solutions

If your cat refuses to use the litter box, there are several ways to address the problem. First, make sure that every cat in the house has his own litter box. The boxes should be separated far enough from each other so that each cat has a sense of privacy. If your other cats are using their boxes but one isn't, try moving that cat's box to a different room. Other cats in the house may be bullying him when he is trying to use the box, and separating them should solve this problem.

If you've recently switched to a different brand of litter, your cat may not like the scent, type, or feel of it on his paws. This can cause him to avoid using the box. Switching back to the old brand

should return everything to normal.

Some cats use the bathtub as their own personal litter box. They may choose to do this because they do not like the litter in the box, because the box is dirty, or because it's the wrong size. To prevent this, leave an inch of water at the bottom of the tub. (This will dissuade your cat from using it.) Place a clean litter box next to it and your cat will get the idea of where he should go. Close the bathroom door to prevent him from going in, and leave a litter box in front of it (or close by). This way, when he wants to "use the bathroom," he'll find a litter box waiting for him.

If your cat has soiled in another area, clean the area thoroughly with a product designed to remove pet stains. Cats can smell where they've eliminated before and will return to the same spot. If your cat keeps returning to this area, make that spot unappealing. Place wide strips of plastic wrap, double-sided tape, or aluminum foil there. Cats do not like the feel of it on their feet and will avoid it. Pet supply stores also sell nontoxic cat repellent that can be used to dissuade them from returning to the same place.

If you catch your cat about to spray or in the process of eliminating, pick him up and place him in a litter box. This will make it clear that this is where he should go. When he uses the box, reward him with lots of loving praise and a treat. If all else fails, after meals, confine him to a small room (such as the bathroom) with a litter box in it. Leave him in there for a few hours or until he uses the box.

If your cat is trying to use the litter box but misses his target, try switching to a covered (or hooded) type, or get a bigger box with higher sides. If it's in a corner, move it out a little so that he can maneuver better, and spread some newspapers around the outside of the box to catch any "accidents."

If you have a large house, your cat might be confused about where the box is. Place a small nightlight near it, and consider putting a litter box on each floor of the house. Cats who have accidents almost always know that they are doing something they shouldn't, but they may be confused about the location of the litter box.

Older cats may have housesoiling accidents because as they age, they lose muscle tone, including muscles that control the bladder. They may not be able to "hold it" until they get to a litter box. If your cat has arthritis, he might need to have a box with lower sides that is easier to climb in and out of.

Remember that if your cat is not using the litter box as he should, something is not right in his world. Although it is frustrating, do not give up on him. Once you do a little investigating and figure out the problem, the solution may be something as simple as buying a different brand of cat litter.

Scratching

It's natural for cats to scratch. They have scent glands located in between their toes that allow them to mark their territory when they do so. If your formerly well-behaved feline is clawing up your furniture, you need to figure out why.

SENIOR CAT TIP

Older Cats With Problem Behaviors

An older cat who engages in an unwanted behavior will need extra time and patience to correct the problem. (The longer the bad habit exists, the longer it takes to break.) If he has a housesoiling problem, consult a veterinarian and schedule a physical. Many older cats become incontinent as they age and cannot control where they eliminate, or they have other problems using the litter box. If the habit is deeply ingrained, he may need to see a behavior therapist and have the unwanted behavior corrected through specific training techniques. Depending on the problem and the age and health of the cat, it may be easier to make certain areas of the house off-limits.

Up a Tree

Causes

One reason that cats scratch where they shouldn't (or didn't previously) is because something in the house has changed, and it is making them feel stressed, bored, or insecure. If you've recently adopted a new cat, the established cat may feel the need to mark his territory to let the new cat know that he is the dominant feline. A new baby in the house or visiting relatives also could stress the cat, and he may vent his frustration on your sofa.

Some cats scratch a piece of furniture that's been brought into the home because it smells different. Scratching to leave his scent behind is the cat's way of making the new chair blend in with the other scents in the house. If you buy furniture at a yard sale or antique store, your cat may smell the previous owner's pet on the furniture and might scratch it to rid "his" house of the

Emotional vs. Physical Problems

If your cat is acting up and you cannot understand why, take him to the vet for a complete physical. In some cases, behavior problems (such as housesoiling) are caused by a medical problem. If the vet cannot find a physical reason for the behavior, then it is likely caused by an emotional upset, and you may want to contact a professional animal behaviorist for advice. Don't just give up on your cat—do everything you can to help him through this difficult time.

other scent. To cure this inappropriate scratching behavior, you need to direct his attention to the one object he should be scratching—his scratching post.

Solutions

If your cat does not have at least one scratching post, get one (or two). This should solve most of the inappropriate scratching problems. Ideally, each cat in the household should have his own scratching post, and it should be in a place he can easily find it.

If you have a scratching post, examine it. Is it worn or all scratched out? If so, it's time for a new post. If the post is new and your cat does not want to use it, rub some catnip along the sides and top. This will attract

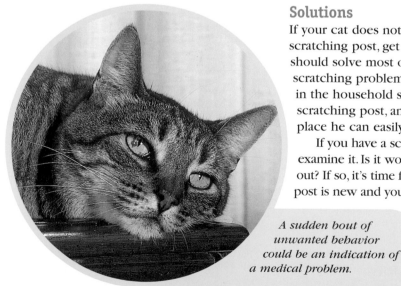

A sudden bout of unwanted behavior could be an indication of a medical problem.

Cats will often misbehave to get your attention.

him to the post, and he'll associate the pleasant scent of catnip with scratching. You also can dangle toys off the top of the post or place treats at the top. The more appealing the scratching post is, the more your cat will use it.

If you catch him scratching something he shouldn't, correct him with a loud "No!" and clap your hands. This will startle him, and he will stop what he's doing. Pick your cat up and move him to the scratching post. Place his front paws on the post and make scratching movements. If he doesn't seem to understand, run your fingernails down the post and pretend

to scratch the post yourself. Praise your cat whenever he uses the post, and give him a treat afterward. He'll make the connection that when he scratches the post he gets rewarded.

To prevent your cat from scratching things when you're not home, cover the edges or corners of the furniture with plastic strips or double-sided sticky tape. Pet product manufacturers sell transparent, nontoxic strips of double-sided tape designed to repel cats without harming them.

Declawing is not an appropriate solution for a scratching problem. Pet supply stores sell little plastic caps that fit over a cat's nails. You can also trim the tips of your cat's nails every few weeks, which will prevent him from clawing anything.

Jumping

Cats are agile and can leap up to five times their height. They like to be in high places to survey the world. Many cats explore off-limits areas when their owners are not home. If your cat is jumping up on places he shouldn't, you can easily train him to stay off those areas.

Causes

Cats are curious and like to explore. Many jump on things to get a better view of the room or to reach a window where they can birdwatch. If your cat is jumping onto the bookcase or chair to look out the window and you don't

mind, that's fine—there's no need to correct him. But if he is jumping on the dining room table during dinner or leaps onto the counter while you're cooking, that behavior should be corrected.

Cats often jump onto places because there's a reward in it for them. If your cat has jumped onto the counter before and found a piece of lunchmeat or cheese, then he's going to return to the counter to see if there's another reward waiting.

Some owners inadvertently create bad jumping habits in their cats. For example, if you let your cat sit on the table when you're paying bills, he will think he can go there all the time—including when you're eating. If you don't want him to jump on the table, don't let him up there at all. If you let him up there sometimes, you will encourage the bad behavior and confuse him about the rules and what's expected of him. Be consistent—if you decide to make something off-limits, it must remain off-limits all the time.

Solutions

If your cat likes to leap onto the counter or table (or anywhere else he shouldn't), make the area as unattractive and unappealing as possible. Pet manufacturers make nontoxic repellents that you can spray in most places. Cats don't like the bitter scent and will avoid it. You also can cover the area with plastic wrap, aluminum foil, or double-sided sticky tape. Or you can always clap your hands loudly, and say "No!" Then pick your cat up and place him on the floor or in his cat condo. Keep doing this until he understands. It's

FAMILY-FRIENDLY TIP

Children and Cats With Problem Behaviors

If your cat has a problem behavior (such as play aggression), teach your children to leave him alone unless he approaches them for attention. An overstimulated cat could frighten or scratch a child. Always instruct children to ask permission from a cat's owner before trying to pet or play with an unfamiliar feline.

always a good idea to show him the "correct" place to sit or jump—such as his cat condo, a chair near a window, or another acceptable area. This is your way of telling him "You don't belong on the counter, but you can sit on this chair."

Do your part to help your cat do the "right" thing. If he goes onto the counter or table in search of a snack, do not leave food out to tempt him and then punish him for doing what's natural (hunting). Some cats like to investigate the sink and will lick leftover food off dirty dishes or pots. If your cat does this, cover the dishes with soapy water. He will quickly decide that it is something he doesn't want to taste. Another solution is to remove the temptation and put the dishes in the dishwasher or wash them right away.

As with children, cats need to learn what the boundaries are in the home. With a little reinforcement and training, you can cure your cat of jumping where he shouldn't.

Biting and Grabbing

If you're playing with your cat and he suddenly rolls onto his back, grabs your hand in his front feet, and starts biting you, you have been the victim of what's called "play aggression." Although this behavior is a natural reaction based on the cat's instinct to stalk prey and defend himself, it's an unwanted behavior that must be corrected.

Causes

Kittens learn to stalk their prey by practicing their hunting skills on their littermates and their mother. They roll around wrestling and even nipping each other. This rough play stimulates the kitten, and he seems to "go wild" kicking his back feet, biting, and clutching "prey" with his front feet.

This is what your kitten (or cat) is doing when he bites or grabs your hand while playing. To some owners, it might be cute to see their kitten "attacking" their hand—but when the kitten grows up, he will continue this habit. You won't find it cute when an adult cat latches onto your hand!

Solutions

To prevent your cat from using "play aggression" on you, never pretend that your hand is a toy and allow him to attack your fingers. Always use a cat-safe toy when playing with him, and he won't see your hand as something that can be pounced on.

If you're playing with your cat and he becomes overstimulated and grabs you, do not pull your hand away. (It will only make him grasp onto you harder.) Let your hand go limp and say "No!" loudly. After a few seconds, he will relax his claws and you can move your hand. Redirect your cat's pent-up energy toward his scratching post or a toy, and let him wear himself out. (This also will show him the "right" objects on which to vent his energy.) After a few moments, he should calm down.

A cat who stalks you and then grabs your ankles when you walk past is also showing a sign of play aggression. Most cats will just grab your ankles with their front paws and hang on for a second,

Cats do not misbehave out of spite; they may simply just be doing things that seem natural to them.

then run away. In this case, the cat isn't trying to hurt you—he's bored and is looking for someone to play with. However, some cats sink their claws in and kick with their back feet. Although they are just playing, this behavior can be unnerving to guests and may frighten small children.

Learn the signs of play aggression so that you'll know when your cat has had enough stimulation. If his ears go flat against his head, his tail puffs up, and he rolls onto his back, stop play immediately and let him calm down.

Other Unwanted Behaviors

Cats are creative and can find many ways to get in trouble around the house.

Some other common feline behavior problems include the following.

Chewing On or Digging Up Houseplants

Cats who eat plants may be looking for extra roughage or greenery in their diet. Buy some cat grass (grass that has been especially grown for cats and that is safe for them to eat) at your local pet supply store and offer it to your cat. It should solve the nibbling problem. If not, spray the leaves of the plant with a mild solution of soap and water or cat repellent. You also can hang your plants from hooks or move them to a place where they can't be reached.

Picking in the Garbage

Some cats like to forage in the garbage can and eat leftovers. Aside from being messy, this habit can be dangerous. Your cat may accidentally come into contact with cleaning products or other poisonous substances, or he could eat bones that could splinter.

If you catch your cat in the garbage, do not rub his face in the trash. Clap your hands loudly and say "No!" Pick him up and move him to another room. To keep your cat out of the trash when you're not around, make sure that the garbage can lid is securely attached or buy a lid that he can't open. You can also move the garbage can to a pantry or hallway or place it in a cabinet under the sink. Another solution is to empty out the garbage before you go to bed. (Most garbage-picking adventures occur in the middle of the night.)

Although behavior problems can be frustrating, do not give up on your cat and decide that he's not worth the time or effort to make him well again. Most cats turned into animal shelters have been given up on by their owners because they have a problem. Sadly, these cats are often considered "unadoptable" and are never given another chance at life. With a little patience, understanding, and reinforcement, you can modify your cat's behavior problems and restore harmony to your home.

Finding a Lost Cat

If your cat becomes lost, act quickly. Any delay in searching for your pet will make finding him harder. Go outside and call his name. (If he does not normally go outside, he will be very overwhelmed and may not leave your yard.) If your cat is trained to come when you call him, he may come running right back to you.

Ask everyone you know to help you look for your pet. Post flyers (with a photo, description, your phone number, and your address) all over the area. Call the local animal shelter or animal control agency, and give them a description of your cat and contact numbers where you can be reached.

Next, call the newspaper and run an ad. Keep looking for your cat on your own, and call local animal shelters and rescue organizations every day to see if anyone has turned in an animal fitting your pet's description.

All cats—even indoor-only cats—should wear a collar with an ID tag at all times. If your pet is microchipped, it will be easier and faster for someone to call a phone number on the ID tag than to find someone to scan for a microchip.

97

Up a Tree

Chapter 8

Stepping Out

There will come a time in your cat's life when you'll have to take him on the road, such as when you need to bring him to the vet's office, but what will you do with him when you go away on vacation? It's a good idea to think about the arrangements you'll have to make if you travel or go away to visit friends or relatives.

Some owners travel with their cats to and from cat shows. If you've never thought about showing your cat, this chapter will give you a brief introduction into the world of cat fancy and give you tips on traveling with your feline companion—wherever your journey leads you.

Showing

Cats have been on display to the public for thousands of years. Ancient Egyptians admired their grace and elegance, and that fascination has continued until today. Cat clubs and "cat fancier" organizations hold local, state, and national shows. If you'd like to show your cat, attend a few events to see if you like them. Many experienced enthusiasts will be there to answer your questions about how the cats are judged and what the different show classes are. Before you whisk your cat or kitten to his first show, ask yourself if he is a good candidate for it.

Should You Show?

Showing your cat or kitten can be a fun and rewarding experience, but only if it's something your cat feels comfortable doing. Not all cats have the right temperament or personality to be a show cat. If your feline is very outgoing, even-tempered, and not upset or made nervous by unfamiliar places, loud noises, or strangers handling him, he'll do well at a show. Show cats need to be complacent and unfazed by the commotion, noise, and goings-on around them.

Most cats who are entered in shows are pedigreed. They are judged against how close they come to the breed standard, which is a specific written description of what the ideal cat in the breed should look like. It includes detailed information about height, body shape and size, coat and eye color, markings, and tail length.

If you don't have a purebred cat, don't worry—you can still enter him in a

Show Preparations

If you've decided to show your cat, take him to the vet for a complete checkup, and be sure he's up to date on all his vaccinations. Show organizers may ask you to provide proof that your cat has a clean bill of health.

The night before the show, bathe your cat and give him a good brushing so that his coat is tangle-free and shiny. Ask a friend or relative to accompany you to the event and act as a "helper" whenever you need an extra set of hands. In addition to your cat and a large crate for him to be displayed in, you need to bring a litter box, food and water dishes, and grooming supplies.

Once you've arrived at the show location, you will be given instructions on what to do and assigned a place to set up. Follow the instructions you're given, but don't be afraid to ask questions if you're confused about something. Enjoy the show!

Before you decide to show your cat, make sure it is something he is comfortable doing.

cat show! Most cat fancy associations allow cats to be shown in one of four categories: Championship, Premiership, Kitten, and Household Pet.

If you're interested in learning more about the world of cat shows, contact organizations such as the Cat Fanciers' Association (CFA), the American Cat Fanciers Association (ACFA), or the American Cat Association (ACA) for information about shows and local cat club chapters. These organizations will be able to tell you how and when you can register for upcoming shows and give you all the details about fees, rules, and the different classes being judged. All

feline registry associations have different guidelines, so do some research and ask questions about the rules, regulations, and requirements for any show in which you plan to participate.

Traveling With Your Cat

If you decide to take your cat with you on a cross-country trip or away for a long weekend, you need to be prepared. Before you pack him up and go, think about his needs. Does he like to travel in the car? Does he get stressed out in new situations, or does he adapt quickly to new places? Evaluate your cat's personality and decide if it's best for

FAMILY-FRIENDLY TIP

Traveling With Children and Cats

When traveling, make sure that your child practices safe behaviors around the family pet. She should be instructed never to take the cat out of his carrier. If you're staying in a hotel or at a friend's house, instruct her to be careful around the cat and never let him go outside (or leave the hotel room). If your cat escapes, he will be frightened in a strange place and may be hard to find. Depending on your child's age, she can help to take care of the cat while traveling by playing with him, brushing or feeding him, or giving him a sense of familiarity and comfort.

him to travel with you. Also, consider where you'll be staying; some hotels and motels do not allow pets.

Before you leave the house, make sure that your cat is wearing his collar with ID tags, and check that the carrier is securely closed and locked. When traveling, stick to his regular schedule as closely as possible. He will not become anxious or stressed if dinnertime and playtime still occur at their usual times. Set aside time each day to play with him and to give him extra attention. The more he feels "at home" while traveling, the more relaxed he'll be. You will also need to make sure you bring along everything that he will need while away from home. The night before you leave, pack his carrier and cat bed; toys; a scratching post; a litter box, litter, and scoop; food; and a brush.

When traveling, place the cat carrier on the backseat of your vehicle and secure it with a seat belt, or put it on the floor. (Do not put the carrier in the trunk!) *Never* leave your cat or kitten unattended in the car for any amount of time. Even with the windows cracked open, the interior of a car can heat up to deadly temperatures in minutes.

Planes, Boats, and Trains

Many owners do not fly with their cats because they feel that pressure changes, crowded conditions, and loud noises are too stressful for them. Some airlines do not allow pets to ride in the cabin of the airplane, and so they transport them in the cargo hold. This can be deadly. Cargo holds are loud and not pressurized, and they're subject to drastic temperature changes. Some pets have died from frostbite or heatstroke while riding in them. Your cat could escape his carrier, and getting lost under these conditions could cause him to suffer psychological trauma. Because of these dangers, many owners refuse to fly on an airline that does not allow pets to travel in the cabin.

Before you buy your plane ticket, ask the airline about its pet policy. If someone tells you that it's okay for your cat to ride inside the airplane cabin with you, make sure that you get the agreement in writing. You don't want any last-minute surprises at the airport.

Before traveling, buy a sturdy, noncollapsible, locking carrier. Your cat should wear his collar and ID tag at all times, and the carrier should be clearly labeled with your name, address, and a phone number where you can be reached while on vacation. Some airlines may require proof of vaccination before they allow your pet to fly. Find out what papers (if any) your cat will need to travel with you.

Trains, buses, and cruise ships all have different rules and policies regarding pets. Before finalizing your travel arrangements, find out if your pet will be allowed to travel with you and under what circumstances.

Home Alone

Depending on your cat's temperament and age, it might be less stressful for him to stay home. If you're only going to be gone for a day or two, you can leave him home alone. However, your cat will become bored and lonely without human companions. If you're going to be gone longer than two days, ask a friend or neighbor to visit periodically and check on the cat. She can play with him, replenish the food and water supply, and tend to the litter box.

Pet Sitters

If you're going on vacation for a week or longer, you may want to hire a professional pet sitter to watch your cat. To locate someone reputable, contact the National Association of Professional

Pet Sitters (NAPPS) at www.petsitters. org. This organization can recommend a cat-loving trained professional in your area. Your veterinarian also may be able to recommend several pet sitters whom clients have used before.

How to Hire a Cat Sitter

If you're going to hire a professional cat sitter, take some time to choose a qualified person, and be sure to do your homework. Above all else, you want to feel comfortable with her and make sure that you trust her with your cat while you're away.

Ask friends, family, coworkers, and your veterinarian for recommendations (as well as any pet sitters to avoid). Interview the top few candidates and ask a lot of questions, such as:

- Is their service a member of the National Association of Professional Pet Sitters?
- How often will they come to your home while you're gone?
- What is the rate, and does the rate vary depending on the number of cats they will be caring for?
- What is their experience with cats, kittens, and older cats?
- Will they give the cat medication if it's required?
- What is their policy for medical emergencies?

Never hire anyone for whom you're unable to get references or recommendations, and make sure that the business is bonded or insured. Arrange to meet the person who will be taking care of your cat. (If the pet-sitting service refuses to let you meet with the person, reconsider using it.) Before you leave, introduce your cat to the pet sitter and see how they get along.

If your cat takes an immediate liking to her, it's a good sign; by the same token, if he despises the person on sight, take that into consideration as well.

The pet sitter whom you choose should like and understand cats. (If at all possible, she should be someone whom the cat knows and trusts.) Leave specific written instructions about feeding times, the amount of food to feed, the general schedule, and any medications that he may need. Give the pet sitter the name, address, and phone number of the vet's office, as well as directions there and a contact number where you can be reached in case of an emergency. Stock up on enough cat food and litter to last until you return.

Boarding

Another option is to board your cat at a pet boarding kennel while you're away. Visit several kennels before you make a final decision. Ask friends and neighbors for recommendations, and research the establishments.

Depending on your cat's personality and condition, it may be better to leave him at home with a pet sitter or a friend rather than board him in a strange place.

When you visit them, ask for a tour of the facilities.

The kennel should look and smell clean, fresh water should be available, and the litter boxes should be relatively unsoiled. Don't hesitate to ask specific questions about the experience and qualifications of the workers, the number of cats being boarded, and the procedures for a veterinary emergency.

Today, there are many modern "cat-only" kennels and boarding facilities (often called "kitty motels") that exclusively board cats in a cozy, home-like setting. These facilities employ people to feed, groom, and play with the cats throughout their stay. Your veterinarian's office also may board cats or may be able to give you several recommendations for reputable places in your area.

Making a Final Decision
Many owners prefer to leave their cat at home with a pet sitter or a friend rather than board them in a strange place. Depending on a cat's personality, he may become stressed if he's taken from familiar surroundings and could feel that he's been abandoned. Always take your cat's feelings into consideration when traveling. Not all cats enjoy a vacation. You'll have a fun-filled trip knowing that your cat is happier being taken care of while you're away.

SENIOR CAT TIP

Traveling With a Senior Cat

Older adult cats or seniors often have a harder time adjusting to travel because they are accustomed to their routine home life. When forced to travel, they may become anxious or stressed. Because of this, be mindful of the temperature in the car (and in the place where you'll be staying). Older cats are sensitive to temperature changes, and your cat could easily become too warm or too cold. If he has a special diet or is on any medications, pack enough supplies to last until you come home from the trip.

Many senior cats do not like to travel (especially if they've never traveled in their younger years) and may prefer to be left home with a trusted family member. Consider the stress and strain that traveling will put on your senior cat, and do what's best for him.

Stepping Out

Resources

Clubs and Societies

American Association of Cat Enthusiasts (AACE)
P.O. Box 213
Pine Brook, NJ 07058
Phone: (973) 335-6717
Website: http://www.aaceinc.org

American Cat Fanciers Association (ACFA)
P.O. Box 1949
Nixa, MO 65714
Phone: (417) 725-1530
Website: http://www.acfacat.com

Canadian Cat Association (CCA)
289 Rutherford Road South
Unit 18
Brampton, Ontario, Canada L6W 3R9
Phone: (905) 459-1481
Website: http://www.cca-afc.com

The Cat Fanciers' Association (CFA)
1805 Atlantic Avenue
P.O. Box 1005
Manasquan, NJ 08736-0805
Phone: (732) 528-9797
Website: http://www.cfainc.org

Cat Fanciers' Federation (CFF)
P.O. Box 661
Gratis, OH 45330
Phone: (937) 787-9009
Website: http://www.cffinc.org

The Governing Council of the Cat Fancy (GCCF)
4-6, Penel Orlieu
Bridgwater, Somerset, TA6 3PG UK
Phone: +44 (0)1278 427 575
Website: http://ourworld.compuserve.com/homepages/GCCF_CATS/

The International Cat Association (TICA)
P.O. Box 2684
Harlingen, TX 78551
Phone: (956) 428-8046
Website: http://www.tica.org

Veterinary and Health Resources

American Animal Hospital Association (AAHA)
P.O. Box 150899
Denver, CO 80215
Phone: (303) 986-2800
Website: http://www.aahanet.org

American Association of Feline Practitioners (AAFP)
200 4th Avenue North, Suite 900
Nashville, TN 37219
Phone: (615) 259-7788
Toll-free: (800) 204-3514
Website: http://www.aafponline.org

American Holistic Veterinary Medical Association (AHVMA)
2214 Old Emmorton Road
Bel Air, MD 21015
Phone: (410) 569-0795
Website: http://www.ahvma.org

American Veterinary Medical Association (AVMA)
1931 North Meacham Road, Suite 100
Schaumburg, IL 60173
Phone: (847) 925-8070
Fax: (847) 925-1329
Website: http://www.avma.org

The Academy of Veterinary Homeopathy (AVH)
P.O. Box 9280
Wilmington, DE 19809
Phone: (866) 652-1590
Website: http://www.theavh.org

ASPCA Animal Poison Control Center
1717 South Philo Road, Suite 36
Urbana, IL 61802
Phone: (888) 426-4435
Website: www.aspca.org

Animal Welfare Groups and Rescue Organizations

American Humane Association (AHA)
63 Inverness Drive East
Englewood, CO 80112
Phone: (800) 227-4645
Website: http://www.americanhumane.org

American Society for the Prevention of Cruelty to Animals (ASPCA)
424 East 92 Street
New York, NY 10128
Phone: (212) 876-7700
Website: http://www.aspca.org

Cats Protection
17 Kings Road
Horsham, West Sussex RH13 5PN UK
Phone: +44 (0) 1403 221900
Website: http://www.cats.org.uk

Feral Cat Coalition
9528 Miramar Road, PMB 160
San Diego, CA 92126
Phone: (619) 497-1599
Website: http://www.feralcat.com

The Humane Society of the United States (HSUS)
2100 L Street, NW
Washington, DC 20037
Phone: (212) 452-1100
Website: http://www.hsus.org

The Winn Feline Foundation, Inc.
1805 Atlantic Avenue
P.O. Box 1005
Manasquan, NJ 08736-0805
Phone: (732) 528-9797
Website: www.winnfelinehealth.org

Websites

Acme Pet Feline Guide
http://www.acmepet.com/feline/index.html
At this site, you can access the feline marketplace for products as well as a pet library, reference materials and articles, questions and answers about cats, an extensive list of rescue organizations, clubs, and shelters, and a "cat chat" room.

ASPCA Animal Poison Control Center
http://www.aspca.org
1717 South Philo Road, Suite 36
Urbana, IL 61802
Phone: (888) 426-4435

Cat Fanciers Website
http://www.fanciers.com
This site offers general information on cat shows, breed descriptions, veterinary resources, and much more.

The Daily Cat
http://www.thedailycat.com
The Daily Cat is a resource for cat owners that provides information on feline health, care, nutrition, grooming, and behavior.

Petfinder
http://www.petfinder.org
On Petfinder.org, you can search over 88,000 adoptable animals and locate shelters and rescue groups in your area. You can also post classified ads for lost or found pets, pets wanted, and pets needing homes.

Pets 911
http://www.1888pets911.org
Pets 911 is not only a website, it also runs a toll-free phone hotline (1-888-PETS-911) that offers pet owners access to important, life-saving information.

ShowCatsOnline
http://www.showcatsonline.com
This online magazine is devoted to all breeds of pedigreed cats. It provides information on breeding and showing and updates members on the latest developments in medical care, breeding, and grooming.

21cats.org
http://21cats.org
21Cats provides information that will help cats live longer, healthier lives. The site contains an online Health and Care InfoCenter, an "Ask the Kitty Nurse" Hotline, and a free monthly newsletter.

Publications

Magazines

Animal Wellness Magazine
PMB 168
8174 South Holly Street
Centennial, CO 80122

ASPCA Animal Watch
424 East 92nd Street
New York, NY 10128

Cat Fancy Magazine
P.O. Box 52864
Boulder, CO 80322

Catnip
P.O. Box 420070
Palm Coast, FL 32142

CatWatch
P.O. Box 420235
Palm Coast, FL 32142

Whole Cat Journal
P.O. Box 1337
Radford, VA 24143

Your Cat Magazine
1716 Locust Street
Des Moines, IA 50309

Books

Toney, Sandra, and Kelli A. Wilkins, *The Simple Guide to Cats*, TFH Publications, Inc.

Wilkins, Kelli A., *The Quick & Easy Guide to Cat and Kitten Care*, TFH Publications, Inc.

Index

Cats

111

About the Author

Kelli A. Wilkins is a multi-published author and a life-long cat lover. Her nonfiction pet care books include *Quick & Easy Cat & Kitten Care*, *The Simple Guide to Cats*, and *Hermit Crabs for Dummies*. In addition to her nonfiction, Kelli has also published three romance novellas with Amber Quill Press and dozens of short stories. She lives in New Jersey with her husband, Robert, and her cat, Inky. Visit her website at: www.KelliWilkins.com.

Photo Credits

Wesley Aston (Shutterstock): 16
Joan Balzarini: 21, 28, 62
Marilyn Barbone (Shutterstock): 46
Linda Beatie: 18, 58
Anne Gro Bergersen (Shutterstock): 85
Mary Bingham (Shutterstock): 30
Mark Bond (Shutterstock): 42, 101
Pam Burley (Shutterstock): 104
Isabelle Francais: 10, 23, 26, 32, 35, 41, 68, 81, 90
Michael Gilroy: 8
Joanna Goodyear (Shutterstock): 49
Shawn Hine (Shutterstock): 89
Aleksejs Kostins (Shutterstock): 70
Gilliain Lisle: 72
Suponev Vladimir Mihajilovich (Shutterstock): 14

Alvaro Pantoja (Shutterstock): 4
Robert Pearcy: 52, 64
Michael Pettigrew (Shutterstock): 78
Robert Redelowski (Shutterstock): 63
Ronen (Shutterstock): 93
Jean Schweitzer (Shutterstock): 98
Vincent Serbin: 37
Claudia Steininger (Shutterstock): 7
TFH Archives: 20, 24, 29, 33, 44, 60, 86, 92, 96
Jeff Thrower (Shutterstock): 9
Trout 55 (Shutterstock): 74, 86
Troy (Shutterstock): 56
John Tyson: 12, 39, 50
Kelli A. Wilkins: 83
Terri L. Zeller (Shutterstock): 76
Tip boxes: Ingret (Shutterstock)
Front cover photo: Jean Schweitzer (Shutterstock)